CW00968496

Dilemmas of Democracy and Political Parties in Sectarian Societies

Dilemmas of Democracy and Political Parties in Sectarian Societies:

The Case of the Progressive Socialist Party of Lebanon 1949–1996

Nazih Richani

First published 1998 by
MACMILLAN PRESS LTD
Houndmills, Basingstoke, Hampshire RG21 6XS
and London
Companies and representatives
throughout the world

ISBN 0–333–73128–X

A catalogue record for this book is available
from the British Library.

10 9 8 7 6 5 4 3 2 1
07 06 05 04 03 02 01 00 99 98

Printed in the United States of America by
Haddon Craftsmen
Bloomsburg, PA

Contents

Preface vii

1. Political Parties in Sectarian Societies 1

2. The Political Economy of Sectopolitics. 15

3. Characteristics of the PSP Leadership,
   Its Composition and Political Behavior 33

4. The System of Domination and the PSP Rank and File,
   Class and Sectarian Composition, 1949–1994. 67

5. The PSP during the Years of Turmoil
   and Reconciliation, 1979–1996. 99

6. The Predicament of Lebanon's Political Parties 107

7. Crossroads between Sectocracy and Democracy:
   The Future of Political Parties 141

Notes 153

Bibliography. 173

Index 181

To all those who lost their lives in sectarian and ethnic conflicts.

Preface

THIS BOOK GREW OUT OF MY DISSERTATION RESEARCH on the Progressive Socialist Party (PSP), which covered the party's development from its inception until 1978. After I finished my dissertation in 1990, I remained interested in following the PSP's development in the years that followed, looking for some sort of closure or a happy ending for my story. This seemed possible with the conclusion of the civil war in 1989, when the PSP and other members of the Lebanese warring factions signed the Taif Accord in Saudi Arabia. Examining PSP behavior for the period 1949 to 1989 and beyond not only provides a comprehensive historical trajectory of the party, but also gives useful insights about the future of Lebanon's democracy and about the role of political parties in the post-Taif era.

With that objective in mind, I conducted field research in Lebanon for eight months between 1992 and 1998. During that time I had the opportunity to conduct another round of interviews with PSP officials, informers, officials of other political parties, and members of parliament. I attempted to explore the prospects of democracy in this battered nation and the expected role of the PSP and other political parties under the Taif regime.

The most important impulse behind this study began when I was a student at the American University of Beirut in the 1970s. I was intrigued by the inability of a party like the PSP to become a "catch-all party" despite its proclaimed secular ideology. More puzzling to me was the PSP's ability to lead the secular forces of Lebanon and champion the cause of democratic reform and social change. These questions led me to investigate the political sociology of the party and its failure to accomplish its secular and national goals while leading the leftist alliance for over three decades. Analysis of the complexities of political development, changes in multiethnic or sectarian societies like Lebanon, and the pressures they bring to bear on political parties provided the answers that I sought.

Of course, this book in its different incarnations was influenced by a great number of people who constantly challenged its basic premises. Without that stimulus this project would have been a rather boring and lonely enterprise. The first person who comes to my mind is Professor Yusuf Ibish, who helped bring the idea of the book into focus and also helped establish the formal contact with Mr. Walid Jumblatt, the leader of the PSP who also was his student at the American University of Beirut. I am also grateful to professors Cynthia McClintock, Bernard Reich, Nathan Brown, and Iliya Harik, who commented on earlier versions of this manuscript. And I am indebted to my friend and editor Ida Oudeh and to my wife, Mona, who not only endured the whole process with me but often offered invaluable criticism and comments. I must also thank a very special group of people—Inaya Balan, Ibrahim Saadeh, Mutaz Dajani, Tarek Nasser, and Hassan Abu Hamze—without their help and emotional support, this work would not have been possible. I should like to express my appreciation to Abido al-Bajha and Issam Lurdi, who facilitated a good number of interviews. I am grateful to my parents, Yasmin and Fouad, for the inspiration and love they have given me. I thank Mr. Walid Jumblatt and the PSP leaders, especially Naim Ghanam, for their help and openness, which allowed the realization of this work.

Finally, I must also thank leaders from the Lebanese Communist Party, Organization of Communist Work , Party of God, Kataib Party, Lebanese Forces, Syrian Social National Party, the National Free Wing, and informants who shared their thoughts and reflections with me.

Chapter One

Political Parties in Sectarian Societies

SINCE THE 1970S the transitions to democracy of regimes in Southern Europe and Latin America have given rise to a plethora of literature on political parties examining the modalities of transition to democratic rule and the role of political parties in the emergence and consolidation of democracy. Yet a central question lingers from the past experiences of democratic breakdowns that has important implications on our evaluation of the current transitions: Why did political parties in the developing countries behave differently than those in the advanced industrial world even when the democratic system was at stake? The Lebanese case presents insights that help explain why political parties behave in certain ways under specific historical circumstances. This book addresses this question within the context of sectarian societies. It explores the predicament of political parties in severely divided societies and their role in democratic development.

Since 1989 Lebanon has been undergoing a period of transition to democratic rule and government. However, its past experience with democratic breakdowns provides valuable lessons that can help us assess the prospects for this particular transition process. Lebanon was arguably the only democracy in the Arab Middle East. Its political parties, such as the Progressive Socialist party (PSP), the Kataib, the Lebanese Communist Party, and others were established prior to the process of modernization, which gathered momentum in the early 1960s. These parties were largely committed to the democratic system and participated in most elections held after Lebanon gained its independence from France in 1943. Paradoxically, these same parties were also instrumental in accelerating the breakdown of democratic politics in 1975. Several questions arise, such as: Why did these parties pursue gun politics instead of democratic practices? Did social distress overwhelm the ability of political parties to organize, compromise, and channel political participation by democratic means?

In answer, this book examines whether the sectarian structure of the Lebanese society and its political system based on sectarian representation limited the ability of political parties to build a constituency that cut across sectarian barriers, and, further, whether such conditions reduced the political choices available to party leadership particularly in times of political and economic distress.

This analysis of the PSP from 1949 to the present is based on three main assumptions: The first assumption is that political parties are organized largely along the same lines as the struggle for political power and resources. If the society is ethnically heterogeneous, then the fight for political power and resources is more likely to assume ethnic overtones, particularly if the unequal distribution of political power overlaps with ethnic lines where one ethnic group dominates the other. Consequently, political parties may play an instrumental role in articulating the ethnic communal "interests." Lebanon's political parties are not unique in this sense; around the world there are many similar examples of parties that represent the political interests of ethnic or confessional groups.[1]

My second assumption is that all societies are divided into classes. As a result, the contestation of political power also is influenced by class interests. Political parties again play an important role in articulating the interests of one or more classes,[2] as the prominent political scientist Seymour M. Lipset asserts: "even though many parties renounce the principle of class conflict or loyalty, an analysis of their appeals and their support suggests that they do represent the interests of different classes."[3]

Thus, this book first identifies the support base of the PSP by examining the class and sectarian backgrounds of more than 17,800 party members. Then it explores the areas in which the party activities were concentrated during the study period. Moreover, in order to establish a link between the PSP political program and its members' class profiles, I shall examine the relationship between changes in the political program and changes in the class backgrounds of recruits from 1949 to 1996.

Third, most heterogeneous societies, whether developed or underdeveloped, are influenced by a combination of class and ethnic politics and interests upon which the political game hinges. To a large extent, political parties in those societies reflect a combination of these two cleavages. Democratic systems can be undermined when class and ethnic deprivation are mutually reinforcing. The Lebanese case is a classic example of this phenomenon.

The scholarship on political parties has dealt with a number of questions that are relevant to this analysis. For example, political scientists Stein Rokkan and Seymour Lipset in their book *Party Systems and Voter Alignments: Cross National Perspectives* examined the extent to which religious differences polarize society when it overlaps with class divisions and how this in turn affects the behavior of political parties. Thus, determining the sets of sociopolitical circumstances which are most likely to favor either accommodations or conflict between political parties become crucial for explaining the political behavior of Lebanese political parties as well as other parties.

VIEWS OF LEBANON'S POLITICAL PARTIES

Very few studies of Lebanon emphasize its political parties. Notable exceptions include John Entelis's study on the Kataib (1974) and Michael Suleiman's more general work (1967). Since these publications, few studies were conducted on Lebanon's political parties; thus our knowledge and understanding is at best speculative. Rather than studying political parties, scholars focused on the analysis of parochial types of political representation based on sect and family, at the expense of more rational and less mundane requirements for elite membership. This focus on the parochial bases of Third World politics has given way to a renewed interest in the agencies and agents instrumental in democratizing societies, a great number of which are in the Third World or in the ex-Communist bloc.

Since its independence in 1943, Lebanon's consociational democracy basically relied on sect leaders and bosses in order to recruit and regenerate the political elite. Thus, political parties played a limited role in Lebanon with the exception of the PSP and the Kataib Party, both of which had some success in bringing new blood into the ruling political elite. This success, however, did not alter significantly the basic way in which the elite was recruited. But the importance of political parties cannot be measured solely by their share in the political elite or parliament, or in the number of portfolios they occupy in cabinets, but also, and more importantly, by their role in the maintenance of a regime's stability and continuity.

This book challenges the assumption that political parties were unimportant in Lebanon's polity and argues that prior to 1975 they were pivotal in maintaining the precarious stability of the political system. The acceptance of the rules of the political game by political parties was vital for the maintenance of the delicate balance of Lebanon's political system, and when this consensus faltered, the regime collapsed. This study demonstrates that the PSP's political behavior was critical both in maintaining the regime and in its subsequent collapse.

I question the popular notion that political parties are an essential element in organizing political participation of social groups generated by modernization. According to Samuel Huntington, a prominent purveyor of this line of argument, political parties facilitate the consolidation of the state and its institutions. In contrast, I argue that the existence of strong political parties is important, but is not sufficient to guarantee political stability, and that one also must look at the greater picture, particularly at the social dislocations created by capitalist development, and at other political conditions that might exacerbate social conflicts. These dislocations and contingencies may accentuate social antagonisms to the point that political parties become manifestations of these conflicts and entangled in conflict dynamics. Thus it is crucial at all times to identify the socioeconomic contexts as well as the contingencies that can affect the behavior of political parties rather than assume in absolute terms that political parties are the essential tools for democratic development; they also can serve as democracy's gravediggers. Under certain historical conditions, political parties do not perform their principal function of linking the public with the state, but can instead exacerbate the sociopolitical polarization that usually accompanies the modernization process.[4] In effect, political parties can serve to delink the public from the state and divide the public along religious, class, ethnic, and regional lines. This situation is particularly likely to occur when state policies fail to redress or ameliorate social hardships and imbalances associated with capitalist development.

In class-divided western industrial nations, political parties have been essential to the maintenance of democracy.[5] Even in cases where class divisions are not the only source of social conflict, such as in the United States, where racial differences play an important role in the polity, political parties helped to moderate racial as well class cleavages. A case in point is the role of the Democratic Party in the 1960s when it incorporated some key demands of the civil rights movement. This helped to reduce social tensions and defused a then-volatile situation. In Lebanon in 1975, Chile in 1973, and Venezuela in 1948, and many others, political parties were unable to iron out their differences for the sake of democratization. This situation led to political breakdowns and military dictatorships in Venezuela (1948-1958) and Chile (1973-1990), and in Lebanon to a civil war, which lasted about fifteen years (1975-1989).

This work departs from the functionalist "problematique" of the late 1950s and early 1960s. In theory, functionalism asks: How do parties function? What is their role in the political system? According to Scott Mainwaring's review of the current scholarship on Latin American political parties, functionalists focus on how parties relate to other leading political actors, particularly the state and other parties.[6] In contrast, my research centers on why political parties relate to other political parties and the state in a certain mode and how this mode in turn could undermine democratic politics. I focus on the structural factors—social, political, and institutional arrangements of power—that influence the behavior of political parties and that are critical to the prospects of democratization and its future consolidation.

This book offers an amended rational choice model wherein rationality and structural factors are both considered pertinent for the analysis of decision making and political behavior. The rational model assumes that actors are motivated by strategic calculations of their interests.[7] To an analysis of these calculations, I add an analysis of: historical contingencies; institutional arrangements (rules of the game that structure power); social and political structures; and the leaders' social backgrounds, ideologies, perceptions, and objectives. First, I will explain the political behavior of PSP leaders in terms of their social backgrounds, political beliefs, and commitment to the rules of the political game and declared objectives. Then, I describe the environmental constraints under which these leaders acted. Third, I assess the political outcome of such behavior, namely the collapse of the democratic system in 1975. Finally, I attempt to predict the behavior of political parties in light of past experiences—particularly if they were to operate under similar structural and institutional arrangements.

As Terry Lynn Karl points out, historically created social and political structures have an impact on the set of alternatives from which political actors may choose.[8] She argues that structural (i.e., power distribution between social groups) and institutional constraints (e.g., the rules of the political game) determine the range of options available and may even predispose political elites to choose a specific option. Karl based her conclusion on a study of pact-making in Latin America. Her argument places the behavior of political parties within a socioeconomic and historical context that underscores the structural bases for decision making.[9]

Many of my conclusions are based on interviews with members of the PSP and other political parties carried out between 1987 and 1996. Beside interviewing more than twenty PSP members who occupied leadership positions between 1949, when the party began, and 1994, I met with twenty-seven informants and officials from the Lebanese Communist Party, Syrian Social National Party (two factions), the Kataib, Lebanese Forces, Popular Democratic Party, Communist Action Organization, General Michel Oun's political movement, Party of God, and independents.[10] I supplemented these interviews with data collected from the records and files of the PSP and other political parties.

POLITICAL PARTIES AND SOCIAL CONFLICTS

Political parties can play an important integrating role in society, as William Chambers demonstrates in his study of American political parties.[11] In several European countries, the question of national integration was largely resolved before political parties appeared on the scene, in the nineteenth century. In Britain, France, Sweden, Norway, and Holland, political parties did not have to confront the issue of nationhood.[12] That was not the case in Germany, Italy, Switzerland, and Belgium, where political parties confronted, to use Myron Weiner and Joseph LaPalombra's phrase, "the crises of nationhood and national identity" at the end of World War I.[13] The construction of "national identities" can explain the precarious interlude in democracy building in these countries in the early decades of this century. The political parties of Germany and Italy stumbled, and their failure to mediate their conflicts led to the emergence of Nazism and fascism respectively. In Belgium and Switzerland, the problems of nationhood and identity were compounded by ethnic and language cleavages. Political parties in both countries had to devise political arrangements to accommodate their social cleavages and a mechanism for mediating conflict.[14] Such agreement between political parties allowed the establishment of consociational democracies that saved both polities from the torturous roads of political turmoil and democratic breakdowns.

In contrast, the record of Third World consociational democracies and the role of political parties is bleaker. In numerous cases, such as Lebanon, Cyprus, Nigeria, Sri Lanka, Colombia, Indonesia, Nigeria, and Venezuela, political parties failed not only to create national cohesion but also to produce enduring political arrangements to sustain their democratic systems. Lipset and Rokkan argued that the establishment of institutional channels for the expression of conflicting interests has helped to stabilize the structure of a great number of nation-states.[15] Most important, for the purpose of this inquiry, is their contention that the effective equalization of the status of different religious denominations has helped to resolve earlier conflicts over religious issues. A second relevant point they highlighted in their influential book, *Party Systems and Voter Alignments*, is the ability of Western industrial democracies to open up channels for the expression of manifest or latent class antagonisms between the privileged and the underprivileged classes. Political parties in the West have been instrumental in building consensus over the rules of the democratic game and, more important, by secularizing politics and moderating class conflicts.

Political parties in the West have a dual and conflicting role, as Robert Alford points out: to unite and to represent group interests.[16] I believe that this is a key element that distinguishes political parties of Western democracies from their counterparts in the Third World. The ability to compromise and mediate conflicts has been tested in countries such as Italy from 1919 to 1923, the first Austrian Republic during its brief existence, the Weimar Republic from 1934 to 1936, and the United States in the decade preceding the Civil War, which led to the collapse of the then existing power arrangements. These failures, however, provided invaluable experience to Western political parties; perhaps the main lesson they learned was how to resolve social conflicts without necessarily sacrificing democratic rule.

The experience of the Western political parties contrasts sharply with that of their counterparts in the Third World, which were, for the most part, established in this century and came to age in the last few decades, with some exceptions in Latin America, where in Paraguay, Colombia, Ecuador, and Nicaragua, a number of political parties trace their origins to the nineteenth century. This time gap between parties of the West and most of those in the Third World could partially explain the differences in the historical experiences of the two groups, particularly in the areas of conflict resolution and conflict management, which are essential in democracy building and consolidation.

The task of building stable democracies is more complex in societies characterized by ethnic and sectarian conflicts. Political parties in fragmented societies largely mirror the social divisions, and under certain circumstances, help to deepen them. Such conditions proved to be detrimental to democracy building and consolidation in some countries. In Nigeria, Sri Lanka, Colombia, and Lebanon, the political parties' social composition largely reflected regional, sectarian, and ethnic cleavages. By appealing to electorates in ethnic and regional terms, and by making ethnic demands on the government, political parties exacerbated regional and ethnic conflicts.[17] All four countries witnessed protracted political violence and the invariable abandonment of democratic principles as a result of the parties' lack of expertise in conflict resolution and mediation on one hand, and their entanglement in ethnopolitics on the other.[18] This condition led a number of proponents of the modernization theory to contend that political parties are to be blamed for ethnic conflicts and antidemocratic movements in the Third World. However, such contentions trivialize the problem by reducing it to the political choice of individual leaders.[19]

This book instead argues that under certain circumstances, ethnic conflicts overwhelm political parties, and more important, some conflicts could undermine the interests and goals of party leadership. Ethnic divisions can be more resilient than party goals and objectives, especially when parties aspire to expand their constituency to other ethnic groups and regions. Donald Horowitz argues along similar lines when he asks: If ethnic conflicts are the creation of political elites, then why do the nonelite follow? To answer that the masses are misled does not square well with the mounting evidence that the masses in Asia and Africa are far from ignorant about politics.[20] Instead, I argue, one must look at how ethnic groups are distributed in the hierarchy of power, how this hierarchy is institutionalized in a given society, and, finally, how the interests of the different ethnic groups are articulated and if this articulation can be reconciled with the interests of other groups.

This research assumes that ethnic contradictions and antagonisms stem from the modes of social and political organization of power. That is to say, understanding of the allocation of political and economic power among the different ethnic groups is pivotal in deepening our knowledge of political struggles and social antagonisms in multiethnic societies. Consequently, I assume that the organization of political power in Lebanon contributed to the limited success of the Progressive Socialist Party to expand its base beyond its native Druze community even when its leadership was earnestly committed to that goal.[21] This assumption, if validated, encompasses a wider set of issues that confronts political parties in fragmented societies. Particularly, it suggests that the choices of the political elite are important but not sufficient to sustain democratization processes.

Yet even when elite consensus is secured, unwanted and unexpected elements(what we call contingencies) can emerge. The Nigerian Second Republic was overthrown at the end of 1983 by a military coup that had little to do with ethnicity or with then-existing consociational arrangements. Similarly, in Sri Lanka the constitutional reforms of 1978 that were designed to enhance the provisions of its consociational democracy were soon challenged by separatists whose grievances antedated the changes.[22] In Colombia, the consociational arrangement of 1958 that officially ended in 1974 but that stayed in effect well into the late 1980s did not pacify the polity; since the 1970s this arrangement came under attack from social groups that the 1958 pact left out. The guerrilla movement representing an important social segment of the Colombian population called for the opening of the political process by changing the constitution and by abandoning the political hegemony of the two-party system.[23] Similarly, Lebanon's political pact of 1943 was challenged by the "nonelite outsiders" and also by a host of regional and international factors that came into play in the internal conflict. These examples cast serious doubts on the argument that interelite agreement is sufficient for maintaining a democratic system.

Horowitz contends that these instances may "suggest that democratic arrangements in conflict-prone societies go awry for reasons so various that the survival of democracy is merely a matter of chance."[24] Although this conclusion provides a bleak forecast about the future of democratization in fragmented societies, it certainly is more sensitive to their social and political complexities than some variants of the modernization theory.[25]

THE MIDDLE EAST AND THE LESSONS OF THIS STUDY

Perhaps one of the core lessons of this study that can offer insight into the Middle East and elsewhere, particularly countries characterized by multiethnic or multisectarian composition, is this: Without a total secularization of their political systems (i.e., in terms of political representation, electoral laws, and composition of their political elites), the chances of democratic development diminish and conflicts are most likely to flare up pending on socio-economic changes and/or contingencies such as foreign intervention. Political parties that emerge in a polarized polity are most likely to reinforce such polarization. A good example is Israel, where almost every ethnic group, including the recently migrating Russians, has its political party (Ysrael Ba-Alyia) to defend its interest against the others. We also can mention the cases of Sudan, Iraq, and Syria, among others.

Sudan's regime slide toward sectarianism since the 1970s has exacerbated the divides between the predominantly Muslim Arab north and the south, which is inhabited by Christians, non-Christians, and Muslims who identify with their African origins. Hence it has drawn the country into a bloody civil war that has ruined its economy and crippled its democratic prospects. Sudan's one-party system, which has increased its intransigence under a type of political Islam espoused by the ruling military junta, has closed the avenue of secularization and polarized the country.

In regional standards, Sudan's political parties were strong and institutionalized (most emerged in the earlier part of this century) and have been gradually marginalized due to the persecutions exercised by the Jaafar Numeiry regime and then after by the new military junta, which banned political parties. Under such conditions, the ability of political parties to articulate an exit from the crisis was largely diminished, and the parties no longer could play a role in ameliorating the sectarian and ethnic divisions precipitated by a sectarian political system whose institutionalized discriminatory power structures circumvent the ability of political parties to aggregate and articulate national interests. Nevertheless, Sudan's political parties must resolve the conflict in the country's southern provinces and reinstitutionalize multi-party secular democracy so that all vital social forces can be an integral part of the political system. In the meantime, the political parties need to avoid the perils of ethnopolitics and its potential damaging effects on future democracy.

Similarly, Iraq's one-party system of the Baath has evolved into a parochial political group centered around Saddam Hussein and his immediate family members and cronies. The Baath, originally a secular political party, became a very exclusive group dominated by a clan. This situation has reduced the party's abilities of co-optation, and contributed to the polarization of the polity. Although traditionally the large Shiite and Kurdish minorities have been traditionally excluded from the political process, the condition has been aggravated further under Saddam Hussein.

The Baath dictatorship has banned and persecuted Iraq's political parties. The marginalization of their political role left space for ethnic groups, sects, clans, and social classes to negotiate their conflicts with the state and among each other by all the means at their disposal, ranging from violence to personal and family ties and alliances.

Syria's brand of the Baath has been less brutal than its Iraqi counterpart; nonetheless, its political parties are kept on a short leash within the National Front, which includes representatives of the Communist Party, the Nasserites, and other groups. The Front is a rubber stamp for the ruling Baath.

Syria's heterogeneous sectarian and ethnic composition (Sunni, Alawi, Druze, Christian, and Kurds) and power structures constitute serious problems for democracy building, particularly if the polity is not secularized and if opportunities are not equally distributed among all groups. Hence political parties are expected to construct a democratic order under discriminatory power structures.

If its political system does not secularize and open up the political process and without discrimination to all citizens, Israel is another case where sectarian and ethnic striving can be expected. The proliferation of ethnic parties on one hand mirrors the heterogeneity of the polity, and on the other hand the inability of the political parties to aggregate the interests of different ethnic groups. Such a condition carries with it the dangers of accentuating social division such as that between secular and orthodox Jew, between Sephardim and Ashkenazi, between recent and old colonizers, and between African Jews and whites. The institutionalized discrimination against the Palestinian population within the state of Israel (and in the occupied territories) exacerbate the divides between the different Jewish groups.

Thus the lack of a secularized state and the complexities of power structures that discriminate against the Palestinians and Jews depending on their places of origins, race, or "authenticity," constitute serious obstacles for the development of democracy. Consequently, political parties in Israel are polarized. This polarization is expected to rise as the prospects of peace with the Arab states and with the emerging Palestinian state in the West Bank and the Gaza Strip increase, especially because some political parties (mostly fundamentalist) are vehemently opposed to the peace process. The outcome of such polarization is difficult to predict at this moment, but the lessons of Lebanon can be insightful.

THE MAP OF THE BOOK

Chapter 2 identifies the social divides that manifested themselves in Lebanon since the nineteenth century and that laid down the framework of the current Lebanese political system. This book demonstrates how sectarian and class divisions found political expression in parties in Lebanon. Chapters 3, 4, and 5 show how the class and sectarian composition of the Progressive Socialist Party changed over time and under what socioeconomic and political conditions.

In chapter 3, I also discuss how the above-mentioned social and political structures influenced the political behavior of the PSP toward the state, other political parties, and democratization. This research slightly modifies Roger Brown's[26] definition of social structure, whereby social structure is the patterned behavior in which each social unit (sect) is seen embedded in a network or web of other social units that respond to it and to whom it responds. Therefore, when I refer to the "social structure" I mean the arrangement of sects according to their status (in the Weberian sense; see chapter 2) and economic capabilities. In turn, I use the term "political structure" to indicate how the arrangement of sects were institutionalized and formalized in the distribution of political power within the state apparatus sanctioned by constitutions, norms, and other political agreements between the members of the ruling elite.[27] Consequently, in this context the "rules of the political game" become the outcome of political and social structures.

I also identify the type of solidarities that were reinforced by the PSP and which ones had to be softened or ignored. Chapters 4 and 5 indicate among which sects the PSP found mobilizing steady support easiest and where it met the most impenetrable barriers of suspicion and rejection.

Finally, chapters 6 and 7 explore the dilemmas of Lebanon's political parties and the prospects of democratization under the Taif constitution. Chapter 7 also sheds light on how the failures of political parties affect the emergence of new civic movements and organizations.

CHAPTER TWO

The Political Economy of Sectopolitics

Let me define from the outset the term "sectopolitics," which I introduce in this book. Sectopolitics is the mobilization of sects on a political basis. It is an ideology that incorporates communal feelings, values, symbols, and the perceptions of an outside threat. It is the political articulation of status interests (sect/religious), and thus seeks to organize political competition between groups along strictly sectarian lines. Sectarianism, which is the term commonly used, means according to *Webster College Dictionary,* the "narrow-minded devotion to a particular sect or religion"; this meaning captures neither the ideological nor the political dimensions of the phenomenon, which made me opt not to use it.[1]

Sectopolitics does not operate in a vacuum; it has agents, such as the state, church, parochial schools, media organizations, research centers, universities, and of course political parties, that participate in making it the dominant ideology in Lebanese society. In this chapter I shall focus only on how sectopolitics became the organizer of the state structures and how it organized the social competition between the different political groups.

Sectopolitics found fertile ground in Lebanese society, which is composed of more than sixteen religious denominations or sects. Lebanon's political parties are divided into main groups. The first group are those parties that professed sectopolitics and consequently are based on the organization of one sect. The second group of political parties are those that adhere to secular ideologies (socialism, nationalism, communism, and others) and seek to build organizations that cross-cut sects. The PSP initially belonged to the second group.

Secular political parties that are born in fragmented societies characterized by sectarian divides such as Lebanon confront three main challenges. One challenge emanates from the society itself with its history of religious conflict and its social groups sharply divided along sectarian lines. The second challenge is posed by the political system, which is based on religious/sectarian representation. The third is that religious and status differences overlap, which makes the struggle for the distribution of resources a mixture of class and status factors. These constitute formidable challenges for the development of secular parties that cut across religious and regional lines. In Lebanon, the Progressive Socialist Party, the Communist Party, the Baath Party, and the Syrian National Party are four secular political parties whose attempt to build parties that cut across confessional lines was met invariably with limited success.[2] This chapter explores the evolution of Lebanon's sectarian system of political representation that came about in the nineteenth century. Understanding the system's origins will help clarify how power came to be distributed along sectarian lines, which paved the way for the establishment of a system of domination built on the superior status of the Maronite elite and the subordinate status of the Muslim political elite.

This chapter situates the analysis of the composition of the PSP within the history of class/religious competition in Lebanon for control of or influence on the distribution of material resources and status since the nineteenth century. I demonstrate that political parties are instrumental in leading the political struggle for the control of the distribution of power and resources. Accordingly, political parties shape and are shaped by the modalities, forms, and distribution of social groups (along ethnic, racial, class, and religious lines, or in any combination of these cleavages) during their competition over resources. Understanding the historical trajectory of such competition and its social basis is a key element in the study of political parties. This chapter demonstrates that Lebanon's sectarian cleavages stem mainly from the class distribution of the social forces in the nineteenth century when the Maronite peasantry played the main role in dismantling the feudal order then dominated by Druze landlords.

THE HISTORICAL ROOTS OF SECTOPOLITICS: LEBANON'S CAPITALIST TRANSFORMATION IN THE NINETEENTH CENTURY

In the mid-nineteenth century the turbulent decomposition of the feudal order was associated with sectarian civil wars, mainly due to the sectarian distribution of the class forces. The predominant class of feudal lords was Muslim Druze, and the majority of peasants were Christian Maronites. The Druze, led by prominent feudal families and with the support of their clergy, enlisted the support of their coreligionist peasants and landlords as well as some Maronites in an attempt to abort the Maronite peasant revolts of 1820, 1821, 1841, 1842, and 1858. These revolts coincided with the period when the Maronite church was expanding its land holdings in the districts of Jubayl, Batrun, and al-Matn to augment its economic resources; this expansion brought the church into clashes with the feudal order and turned it into a peasant ally.

What helped the Maronite church was the reforms that it underwent in the eighteenth century, which equipped it to play an instrumental role in the downfall of the feudal order. In 1736 a church council introduced radical reforms in church organization and structure. These reforms aimed at restricting the influence of the Maronite feudal lords in church affairs, particularly in prelate nominations. Lay notables were allowed to present candidates for clerical functions only, while the actual nomination was limited exclusively to the clerical hierarchy. Prior to these reforms, feudal families such as the Khazin family in Kisirwan (a Maronite stronghold) exercised virtual control over the election of patriarchs and the nomination of ecclesiastical dignitaries, particularly *mutrans* (metropolites). According to then existing practice, no patriarch could assume his function without the blessing of the Khazin landlords.[3] The Maronite aristocracy resisted these church-imposed changes simply because they challenged their feudal authority. This situation in effect led to the separation between the Maronite church and the Maronite aristocracy (and by and large with the feudal order) in the eighteenth century, a separation that grew into a complete divorce in the nineteenth century.

When in the 1800s the peasants started revolting against tax increases levied by the landlords *(muqataaji)*, the church was organizationally prepared to play a leading role in dismantling the feudal order and was motivated because doing so could enhance its political and economic fortunes. Thus the church was on a collision course with the feudal system and its symbols, particularly the Druze landlords. The church expanded its power base, with the peasants constituting the largest pool from which it drew its clergy and labor to exploit the land. The church developed a cheap and profitable enterprise by establishing monastic religious associations, called the Lebanese Order, in different localities. Historians estimate that in the nineteenth century, the Maronite church became one of the largest landholders in Mount Lebanon, and the Lebanese Order became the largest agricultural enterprise in the area.[4] Interestingly, the Lebanese Order provided a new centralized system of finance and management of agricultural land. It represented a prototype for agribusiness and the mode of capitalist production characterized by wage labor.[5]

The revolt of 1820, a protest against rising taxes and the ruthlessness of feudal landlords, was led by lower—and middle-class clergymen under the leadership of a Maronite bishop, Yusuf Istefan (1759-1823), and directed against Bashir Shihab, the Ottoman-appointed ruler of Mount Lebanon (a Sunni who converted to the Maronite faith), and Bashir Jumblatt, a Druze feudal leader.[6] In 1821, 1841, 1842, and 1857 revolts also took place; they were more democratic in character, in that their leadership was elected from the commoners and clergy. During the 1857 peasant revolt, led by an elected peasant named Tanoius Shaheen, Maronite peasants confiscated the lands of the Maronite Khazin feudal landlords, ceased to pay taxes and tributes, and declared their intention to destroy the feudal order itself.[7] This was too radical for the Maronite church and to the foreign European powers who were watching the development of the revolts closely. The situation climaxed in 1860 after several decades during which the Druze feudal lord (and their junior Maronite feudal lords allies) resisted the socioeconomic and political changes pressed by Maronite peasantry and priesthood. The 1860 civil war was a bloodbath, which left 15,000 Christians dead, and left 100,000 homeless. (No figures are available on Druze casualties.)[8]

Although this description of the conflicts in the nineteenth century is greatly simplified, it captures the essence of the struggle between the Druze and the Maronite communities for political and economic supremacy. What is relevant for our inquiry is that the socioeconomic transformation of the nineteenth century was associated with religious political polarization between the Maronites and the Druze.

Such political polarization tended to define the grounds of the contestation of political power and the competition for resources throughout most of the 1800s; in addition it was instrumental in determining the political parameters of that competition in modern Lebanon. The Double Kaimakameih (district) and the Mutasarafiah political regimes of the nineteenth century were prototypes of the 1943 political system.

THE DOUBLE KAIMAKAMEIH AND THE MUTASARAFIAH REGIMES: THE PROTOTYPES OF THE 1943 REGIME

The Kaimakameih system was established in 1842 in the wake of the peasant revolts, in an attempt to introduce tranquility into Lebanon. The political and economic rivalries between the Maronite church, the main supporter and benefactor from the peasant revolts, and the feudal Druze landlords who managed to rally the support of Druze peasantry created constant tension and conflict. The peasant revolts also coincided with the increase in European political, cultural, and economic penetration of Lebanon and the region at large.

By the mid-nineteenth century, the French had developed strong cultural, political and economic ties with the entrepreneurs and Maronite Church. The British colonizers tried to forge similar ties with the Druze feudal lords. As a result of these ties, the European powers started meddling in the affairs of the Mount Lebanon as part of their struggle to inherit the fortunes of the crumbling Ottoman Empire. They were preparing the ground for its dismemberment when the time was ripe.

That period marked the beginning of direct European intervention in Lebanon's internal politics. The Double Kaimakameih system came at the conjuncture of civil strife, foreign intervention, and the weakening of the Ottoman rule; it led to the division of Mount Lebanon into two districts *(Kaimakameih),* one ruled by a Maronite and one by a Druze. This division of political power ushered in institutionalized sectarianism, (i.e., sectopolitics). This arrangement was made to correspond with the religious distribution in each district. The *Kaimakam* (governor) of each district was assisted by a council composed of an advisor and judge from each of the Sunni, Druze, Maronite, Greek Orthodox, and Greek Catholic communities, plus just an advisor from the Shiite community, since the Ottomans did not recognize the Shiite as having a separate magistracy.[9] Council members became their sect political representatives.

The Mutasarafiah came in the aftermath of the peasant revolt of 1858, which escalated in 1860 into a religious war between the Maronite and Druze. The Mutasarafiah, a more advanced formula of governing, replaced the Double Kaimakamieh and called for the unification of Mount Lebanon into one district that would be ruled by a single governor, a Mutassarif. This new arrangement was negotiated by the five European powers—France, Britain, Russia, Austria and Prussia—with the Ottomans. Although the pact did not specify the Mutassarif's religion, in practice a non-Lebanese Ottoman Christian was selected with the consent of the five European powers.

The Mutasarafiah system again reinforced the sectarian mode of political representation by creating a Central Administrative Council composed of twelve members—four Maronite, two Greek Orthodox, one Greek Catholic, one Sunni, one Shiite, and three Druze—representing their sects. Two main paradoxical achievements can be attributed to the Mutasarafiah system: In spite of its formal abolishment of feudalism, it allowed feudal families to keep their possessions and wealth and to retain their power as district rulers, administrators, and members of the Central Administrative Council.[10] Some of these families, such as the Jumblatt and Arislan, conserved their power and influence to this day.

The Mutasarafiah system was dissolved in 1915 by the Ottoman Empire when it entered World War I. After the defeat of the Ottomans, Lebanon (like most parts of the empire) came under French and British colonial control. In 1920 the French created Greater Lebanon, which in addition to Mount Lebanon included the Biqa', Tripoli, and South Lebanon. The new regions were inhabited predominantly by Sunni and Shiite communities. The Maronite became the largest sect; the Sunni became the second largest sect followed by the Shiite; the Druze became a minority group.

Right after the French occupation of Lebanon—under the League of Nation's Mandate—a French governor was appointed, to be assisted by an advisory council drawn from Lebanese notables who represented all religious sects. In 1922, the French governor Gouraud, decreed the institutionalization of the Representative Council from the various sects. Subsequently, this council promulgated the 1926 Constitution that has defined the parameters of political life in Lebanon ever since. One of the main features of the 1926 Constitution was its acceptance of sectarian/ religious representation as the main form of political representation; thus it defined Lebanon as an association between sects.

Although the constitution provided the political framework for the system, it was not sufficient to settle the interelite conflict over the specifics of the sectarian distribution of public office and over the future of Lebanon as an independent state. That goal was accomplished by the ill-fated National Pact of 1943, which formally divided political power between the major religious groups. Another important objective of the National Pact was the drawing of a compromise between the Pan-Arabist segment of the elite (which was calling for a unity with Syria) and a Maronite faction, which called for a Maronite ministate in Mount Lebanon under the protection of France. Bechara el-Khoury, a Maronite who was elected president in 1943, and his Sunni prime minister, Riyadh al-Sulh, a popular pan-Arabist, were instrumental in brokering the pact, which finally resolved (temporarily, at least) the conflict between the two factions. The pact was based on the notions that Lebanon should be completely independent, sovereign and neutral; that the Christians, and especially the Maronites, should not seek Western protection; and that the Muslims, especially Sunni, should not try to make Lebanon part of an Arab state.[11]

The National Pact stayed in effect until 1989, when a new political pact was signed in Taif, Saudi Arabia, between the warring factions. The Taif accord maintained the sectarian system of political representation and stipulated the equal distribution of public office between Christians and Muslims. The accord also expanded the number of seats in parliament from 99 to 118, divided equally between Muslims and Christians. In a sense the Taif Accord is merely an updated version of the 1943 National Pact; it made explicit what had been generally a norm with a slight change reflecting the new demographics of the Muslim population.

THE OVERLAP OF CLASS AND SECTARIAN CLEAVAGES

Dietrich Rueschemeyer, Evelyne Stephens, and John Stephens argue that race and ethnic divisions acquire importance when they are linked to class and/or where racial and ethnic groups are differentially linked to the state apparatus.[12] When ethnic divisions overlap with class divisions, they can damage democratic politics more than when class and ethnicity differentiations are not aligned. The authors cite Belgium and Switzerland as examples to illustrate two cases where deep ethnic divisions are not aligned with class divisions, a condition they believe allows these countries to maintain consociational democracy. The authors also note that the state apparatus may differentiate between the different ethnic groups on the basis of quotas, as is the case in Lebanon, where representation in public office is based on a ratio of six to five in favor of Christians. This system of sectarian representation was based on the 1932 population census (the only census ever made), which established that the number of Christians exceeded the number of Muslims by the same ratio. Consequently, the Maronite political elite and bourgeoisie occupied a comparative advantage in the state apparatus and controlled the distribution of resources. The alignment between sect and class in the distribution of wealth and political power is central for our analysis of Lebanon's sectarian conflict. It helps explain some of the root causes for the limited success of the PSP (and other secular political parties) in building national organizations that cut across sectarian divides.

Max Weber argued that political parties may represent interests determined through class/status conditions, and they need be neither purely class nor purely status parties. According to Weber, most parties are partly based on class and/or status interests. He observed that political parties may differ in their social base and political program according to whether the community is stratified by status or by classes. Above all else, he contended, political parties vary according to the structure of power and domination within the community.[13]

Weber defined the condition of status as "every typical component of the life fate of men that is determined by a specific, positive or negative, social estimation of honor."[14] Religion could help in building group solidarity based on a common set of beliefs, values, symbols, rituals, and more important, a common fate. This form of group solidarity acquires additional functions when it is linked formally with the state structures and becomes sanctioned by laws or norms. In fragmented societies, Weber argued, status groups (ethnic, religious, and race) could become structured into a vertical social system (hierarchy) of superordination and subordination. He thought that such social structures approximated the caste system, which brings about a social subordination and an acknowledgment of "more honor" in favor of the privileged caste and status groups.[15] These Weberian propositions are important for the sociopolitical study of the PSP and lay down the theoretical linkage between the social composition of a political party and the general structure of domination in society.

In Lebanon, the formation of status structures was intrinsically related to the political structure of power. The National Pact of 1943 assigned the Maronites "more honor" (i.e. more status vis-à-vis the other sects) in terms of the distribution of political power. They were given the key positions of the presidency of the republic, the army chief, the command of the intelligence apparatus, and other.

The status system in Lebanon was based politically on the Lebanese constitution of 1926, which stayed in effect until its amendment in 1990, and the unwritten National Pact of 1943. The constitution stipulated in its provisional Article 95 that for reasons of "amity and justice," government posts and public office positions should be equitable between the different religious groups. Although the article was introduced as a provisionary measure to quell sectarian differences, the political elite failed to amend it more than forty years after Lebanon gained its independence. Over the years the Maronite political elite and the Christian bourgeoisie succeeded in exploiting their access to state resources granted to them by the National Pact (principally through the key position of the presidency) in the absence of an efficient checks-and-balances system.[16]

Although Lebanon is a constitutional parliamentary republic, the presidency has acquired institutional power vested by the constitution. After independence, its presidents succeeded in establishing for themselves a hegemonic position within the ruling class. The constitution states that the president names the prime minister who in turn selects the cabinet. In theory, the cabinet is answerable to the parliament, but in fact it is answerable to the president. The Lebanese people elected a parliament every four years (until 1972, the last election prior to the 1975 civil war; elections resumed in 1992); the parliament, in turn, elects the president of the republic for a nonrenewable six-year term. However, the constitution stipulates that the President is given other powers that can be exercised only with the approval of the council of ministers (over which he presides), such as dissolving the chamber and calling for general elections. He can postpone the convention of the chamber for a month, or he can ask the chamber to convene in a special session. He also can veto bills passed by the chamber, and his veto can be overridden only by two-thirds majority.[17] In practice, the power to appoint and dismiss the prime minister and his cabinet has provided the president with ample power to achieve his political agenda.

In this sense the presidency constituted the most powerful position in Lebanon's political structure, and thus it provided the Maronite Christians with superior status in the power structure. Moreover, the presidents also played a significant role in advancing the class interests of their class/sect groups.[18]

THE ALIGNMENT OF SECT AND CLASS DOMINATION

Perhaps if sect and class domination had not been aligned, the competition over resources would have been less conflictual and bloody. Foreign interference and the relative weakness of a multiconfessional bourgeoisie in the nineteenth century were two factors that positioned the Maronite Church at the helm of the capitalist transformation process. This allowed the Maronite and Christian entrepreneurs and merchants to occupy a better position in the new socioeconomic and political order. This explains why the bourgeois class was drawn largely from the Christian communities, a situation that lasted for most of this century. Three studies conducted between the late 1950 and the early 1970s support this point. Economist Yusuf Sayigh, who analyzed the religious/sect composition of the entrepreneurial class in Lebanon in the early 1960s, suggested that the Christians had an earlier start than the Muslims and succeeded in maintaining their lead into the 1960s. The Christians owned most of the industries in all sectors.

Another study performed in the early 1970s concluded that the trend had not been reversed; Christians owned twelve of the twenty-five largest industrial enterprises in Lebanon, and they own the majority of shares in five others. The Sunni bourgeoisie owned three industrial firms and had the majority of shares in five. The Druze and the Shiite bourgeoisie were both underrepresented in this sector.[19] This fact suggests that until the early 1970s, the Christian bourgeoisie occupied a dominant position in terms of its ownership of the means of production. The Christians owned 75 percent of the commercial sector whereas the Muslims owned about 25 percent.[20]

Joseph Chamie's 1971 study of the distribution of income and occupation by religious/sect reported the income, and occupational and educational differentials between Christian and Muslim communities. Chamie found that Christians in general earned higher incomes and occupied more prestigious, well-paying professional/technical positions than Muslims. For example, the proportions in the professional/technical sector versus the labor sector are as follows per sect : 2 percent versus 35 percent labor(Shiite); 4 percent vs. 23 percent (Sunni); 3 percent vs. 20 percent (Druze); Catholic (predominantly Maronites) 6 percent vs. 18 percent; and (non-Catholic Christians) 6 percent vs. 16 percent.[21]

Clearly, the social and economic differences between the sects put Christians at the top of the social pyramid, Druze around the middle, Sunni near the bottom, and Shiite at the very bottom.

During the 1990s the religious composition of the bourgeois class witnessed some changes but the Christian predominance within this class was not altered. The largest industrial—of 100 workers or more—and trading enterprises are still owned by Christians. In the financial sector however, some advances were made by the Sunni and Druze bourgeoisie; the Shiite remained outside the club of the ten largest banks. The Sunni bourgeoisie possess the majority of capital in three of the largest banks, the Druze in one, and the remaining six are predominantly owned by the Christian borgeoisie. In the contracting sector the Sunni and the Shiite have made some strides. In the service sector however (restaurants, hotels, and wholesale), the Christians have retained their traditional stronghold.[22] In this sense, despite some structural changes in the sectarian composition of the Lebanese bourgeoisie, the Christians still enjoy a preponderance over their Muslim partner.

SECTS UNDER THE LAW

Another important aspect of the historiography of sectopolitics and its current manifestations is the law of personal status. Each of Lebanon's seventeen religious sects struggles to maintain its identity and autonomy.

These aims are facilitated by the development of parallel, but separate, legal and social institutions. According to Article 9 of the constitution, each sect is entitled to organize its own legal codes regarding the family laws. The sects are in charge of their own courts and enjoy the sole authority over matters of divorce, marriage, inheritance, separation, adoption, and tutelage. Lebanon does not have civil courts that deal with personal status matters.

Moreover, according to Article 10 of the constitution, each sect controls the education of its children. This has led some sects (starting with the Christian ones), to establish their own elementary, middle, and secondary schools. In light of the very loose guidelines placed by the Ministry of Education, sects enjoy virtual autonomy in deciding their curriculum and educational materials. This situation led to different versions of the historiography of Lebanon with each sect trying to undermine or highlight certain aspects of history to serve parochial, ideological, and political interests. This confusion in the reading and interpretation of Lebanon's history was eloquently discussed by the Lebanese historian Kamal Salibi in his book *A House of Many Mansions.* Salibi argues that the different versions of history presented mainly by the Druze and Christians are indicative of the sectarian divides that prevented historians from writing an objective historical account above sectopolitical interests.[23] Such controversies exacerbated the religious differences and increased the fragmentation of the political culture. More important, generations of Lebanese are socialized to different sectarian interpretations of their country's history; they are fed on with the grains of sectarian segregation and suspicion of the "other." In this respect, religious schools have been instrumental in the fragmentation of the political culture and in the fomentation of sectopolitics. Furthermore, their pervasiveness has undermined the development of a national public school system and a unified educational system in Lebanon.[24] It is important to keep in mind that over the years religious schools acquired a strong and influential lobbying power that was instrumental in defending their territories. These schools acquired additional importance during the war, 1975 to 1989, when public schools and universities (as well as most state institutions) reached the point of virtual collapse.

Lebanon's religious segregation also included most social organizations, sport clubs, charitable organizations, and cultural groups, which were largely constructed along sectarian lines. Furthermore, sects in Lebanon are concentrated in specific areas; the Maronites, for instance, live in certain areas such as the Zgharta, Kisirwan, and the Batrun districts; the Druze are in the upper Matin, Shouf, and Hasbia in Biqa'; the Sunni are the majority in Tripoli, Akkar, Sidon, and Beirut; and the Shiite constitute the majority in South Lebanon and the Biqa'. This concentration of sects in specific areas added to the religious cleavages by creating physical and psychological barriers between sects in addition to the ideological-institutional barrier, sectopolitics. The sectarian demographic distribution coupled with disparities in the development of the regions have grown in the years since independence and thereby added more fuel to the flames of sectarian conflict.

PARALLELS WITH THE WESTERN POLITICAL EXPERIENCES

Political parties that were established in such a fragmented environment confronted the difficult task of overcoming sectarian barriers. Most of the secular political parties have had limited success in building catchall parties that represent proportionately the cross-section of the populace.

It is not a novel discovery to say that social divisions would produce political parties. Lipset and Rokkan viewed social divisions as expressions of the socioeconomic and political strains associated with capitalist development. Most European and North American political parties reflect class differences, pitting an often socialist, anticlerical and working-class based left against a more middle-class and business-oriented right.[25]

Acute social class struggles in the industrial countries were pervasive until the societies succeeded in instituting welfare states underscored by social pacts and economic growth which trickled down to the working class, and thus, triumphed in changing the modality of class antagonisms. Workers and parties that represented them toned down their demands in the 1950s and early 1960s. The 1970s ushered in the beginning of the postindustrial revolution, which created new social forces and eliminated others; a new left and a new right emerged that based their programs and demands on changing social interests.[26] In the 1980s another wave of political groups emerged, responding to new social strains such as the Green Movement, ethno-regionalist parties in Europe, the Ross Perot and Sylvio Berlusconi phenomena in the United States and Italy respectively. If there is a common denominator among the new political movements and parties in the postindustrial West, it is that as Peter Drucker wrote in his book *Post-Capitalist Society*, knowledge has become the resource rather than a source; this is one of the main characteristics of postcapitalist societies. According to Drucker, this "changes fundamentally the structure of society. It creates new social and economic dynamics. It creates new politics."[27] This new politics is certainly based on new social interests generated by the transformations in the socioeconomic spheres and is increasingly making traditional political parties look obsolete. It is important to keep in mind that these transformations took place in the developed nations against the backdrop of a nearly two-century-old tradition of church-state separation.

In sharp contrast, Lebanon has yet to secularize; the church/mosque plays a dominant role in the state and society. Sectarian divisions that have been institutionalized since the mid-nineteenth century remain largely ossified in a political system that is unable to adjust to socioeconomic and political changes and transformations.[28] The sectarian system of political representation became a major source of social strains when the Christian Maronite community lost its numerical superiority over the Muslim sects. The inability and the unwillingness of the Maronite political elite to relinquish part of its political privileges exacerbated sectarian divisions.[29]

This condition made it impossible for secular parties of the left to ignore or overcome the effects of sectarian divisions, particularly since the Muslim community came to constitute the majority of the underprivileged social classes. For example, political parties such as the Communist Action Organization claimed that there is a ruling class/sect in Lebanon in which the Maronite elite rules in the name of the dominant class and dominant sect in society.[30] The Lebanese Communist Party, on its part, established a close alliance with the Muslim elite particularly after 1975, incorporating Muslim demands to expand Muslim representation in government.[31] Consequently, the Muslim community and other non-Maronite Christians tended to be more supportive to leftist and liberal political groups than the Maronite community. This trend reveals the importance of sectopolitics and how it affects some main party's programs, behavior, and membership, something that political parties in Western democracies have avoided due to the secularization of their polities and the rationalization of their economies by the introduction of the welfare state.

Political parties of the right such as the Kataib (founded in 1936 by Pierre Jumayyel) and the Lebanese Forces (the umbrella military organization that included the Kataib and other parties emerged during the 1975-1976 civil war) are predominantly Maronite organizations with no desire to expand their constituency beyond the Christian community whose interests, values, and way of life they claim to safeguard.[32] The role of these sectopolitical organizations was reinforced by the key role played by the Christian Maronite church and its associated organizations, schools, and universities. In retrospect, the political outcome was the creation of solid Maronite support behind the political system and the then existing system of domination (1943-1989). This fact partially explains the weak support that the secular parties received from the Maronite community.

Another contrast with the Western political experience is the sectarian political framework of the system that defined the parameters of political rivalry and competition for political power and control of the distribution of resources. Members of parliament, for instance, acted as representatives of their sects; they were expected to defend its interests and expand its access to state resources and monies. The construction of a road in the remotest villages was subject to sectarian wheeling and dealing among members of the elite. Their discourse was drawn largely along according to sectarian lines.

A representative example of the type of political exchange between deputies is one speech delivered by parliament member Rashid Baydoun, son of a prominent Shiite traditional family, in 1943:

> Give the Shiite their rights in jobs and education, construct the roads in their [Shiite] villages improve the standards of living of their workers and peasants. . . . We [Shiite] want our rights from this independence in which the Shiite paid with blood [in reference to those killed in confrontations with the police forces] more

> than any other sect for its achievement. Yesterday a position was vacated by a Christian Catholic and they claimed that this position should be only filled by Christian Catholic. Where are the high ideals? Where is the gratitude to the Shiite who sacrificed their lives for the cause of independence?[33]

In this system of sectarian representation, members of parliament are responsive mainly to their constituency/sect. The deputy's role is to articulate the political interests of his sect, and his record of success is measured by how many "resources" he secures for his religious group; how many people he succeeds in employing in private or public sector; the number of schools, hospitals, and services (such as telephone lines and roads) he secures for his area. Although these functions sound typical, in Lebanon they are geared to the benefit of the sect. The different deputies compete aggressively for limited resources in order to advance the interests of their sects and regions. Such competition succeeds in maintaining sectarian polarization in the country for most of the post-independence era.

Political debates in the parliament and the exchanges between deputies and political leaders are loaded with sectarian undertones. This political environment contributes to a heightened sectopolitical consciousness among the populace, grounded in the belief that groups are defined along sect/religion lines and are engaged in a zero-sum political game. The Muslim community perceived the Christian community as the dominant political group occupying a privileged position in Lebanon's power structure, and thus exercising more influence and control over the allocation of state resources. Many Muslims believed that Christian used state resources at the expense of the Muslim community, and in turn the Christians feared that Muslims are trying to undermine their political power in order to seize complete control.[34]

Michael Hudson argues convincingly that socioeconomic and political structures do not fully explain the rivalry between Christian and Muslim communities; both groups also have different systems of beliefs and values and are profoundly concerned about the possibility that rival sects may gain power at their expense.[35] The political system and its institutions heightened this rivalry through its sectarian representation, and reinforced the differences in values by assigning the church/mosque an independent role under which each practiced monopoly over personal laws, schools, and the like. This account of the social and historical foundation of sectopolitics, although far from complete, is essential for our understanding of the political and sociohistorical environment under which the Progressive Socialist Party was established in 1949

CHAPTER THREE

Characteristics of the PSP Leadership, Its Composition and Political Behavior

AMID THE COMPLEX POLITICS of a deeply fragmented society, the Progressive Socialist Party (PSP) was founded in 1949 by a group of young leftist intellectuals who were genuinely interested in social democratic secular change. But, as this chapter demonstrates, their intentions were far less resilient than the society's and polity's resistance to secular change. Here I address three core questions: (1) Why did the leadership of a secular party like the PSP fail to develop a multiconfessional organization? (2) How did Lebanon's major political crises influence the sectarian and class composition of the PSP leadership? (3) And finally, in what ways did the PSP leadership contribute to the breakdown of the consociational democracy in Lebanon?

The structure of power in Lebanon is a key independent variable in this research. It is defined as the mode of distribution of political resources among the different sects. In Lebanon this distribution was set in accordance with the 1926 constitution and the unwritten National Pact of 1943, which assigned to every sect a given status in the hierarchy of power. The distribution of power among the different sects is mediated by a host of factors ranging from the type of electoral system in place to the dominant ideology in the Lebanese society, namely sectopolitics. Sectopolitics legitimate the sectarian political system by claiming and promoting its positive attributes and uniqueness.

The PSP leadership failed to extend its power base beyond the Muslim Druze community due to the above-mentioned structural and institutional variables. These independent variables have shaped the menu of choices, alternatives, and incentives available to the PSP leaders, particularly in times of political crises. This chapter investigates the structural and political conditions (within and without the PSP) that influenced the political choices made by PSP leaders during two main crises situations: the 1958 revolt and the 1975 civil war. These crisis situations represent two instances where the PSP leadership took political decisions that contributed to democratic deadlock and to the breakdown of the political system.

Not withstanding the impact of structural and institutional variables on the range of choices available to political leaders at times of crisis, this research invokes the cautionary notes of Juan Linz[1] and Arturo Valenzuela[2] against sociological determinism. They cautioned that politics is not static; variables such as leadership roles must be considered and the dynamics of the political process must be analyzed in explaining complex phenomena such as political breakdowns. Linz and Valenzuela consider that the "structural characteristics of a society, the actual and latent conflicts, constitute a series of opportunities and constraints for the social and political actors, men and institutions which can lead to one or another outcome. . . . these actors have certain choices that can increase or lower the probability of the persistence and stability of a regime."[3]

Here I explore how the structure of power and the choices of the PSP elite correlated with the dynamics of a changing socioeconomic and political environment. My analysis is based mainly on interviews with PSP officials that I conducted in Lebanon in late 1987, 1988, 1989, 1992, 1994, and 1996. This case study approach provides qualitative data that allowed me a close and in-depth look at the "black box" of the PSP decision makers, without excessive bias to some variants of the rational choice model which underrate structural variables and/or overlook intervening variables.[4]

To what extent did social and political structures in Lebanon help in shaping the class and religious configuration of the PSP leadership? To answer this question, I analyze the changes in the social class and religious backgrounds of the leaders that assumed leadership roles from 1949 to 1994. I also identify the ideological and political orientation of more than a dozen prominent PSP members who held leadership positions during the study period. While this research also assesses the party leaders' personal motivations in joining, it does not claim to present conclusive findings about their motives. However, it attempts to provide a fair close-up that approximates reality.

It is important to mention here that the PSP hierarchy is made up of three tiers: leadership council, advising members, and working members. The leadership council is the highest authority within the party and is elected by the general assembly of advising members and representatives of the branches and regional leaders. The advising members are the second-tier leaders and act as advisors to the leadership; from their ranks the leadership council members are drawn.

THE GENESIS OF THE PARTY

Kamal Jumblatt was born in 1917 in the castle of al-Moukhtara in the heart of the Shouf on the serene slopes of Mount Lebanon. Jumblatt's family had been one of the leading feudal families in these mountains since the seventeenth century. Since then the Jumblatt clan has been omnipresent in the power structure of the Druze and by extension in Lebanon's politics up to the present. Kamal Jumblatt inherited the leadership of the clan after the death of his brother-in-law and cousin, Hikmat Jumblatt, who was a member of the National Bloc, a parliamentary caucus formed by a pro-French Maronite headed by Emille Edde. At the insistence of his mother, al Sitt Nazira Jumblatt, he followed in his predecessor's footsteps and joined the National Bloc. In 1943 he was elected to the Lebanese parliament as a National Bloc member, thereby entering politics from the traditional route.

In 1941, however, two years prior to his election, Jumblatt started voicing radical ideas. In a speech at a reception for General George Catreux, the French commander of the allied forces in Lebanon, Jumblatt spoke with such great zeal about the wretched life conditions of the peasants and about the working- class exploitation that one French official labeled him a socialist.[5] Jumblatt's exposure to socialist ideologies started during his study in France in the late 1930s, when he joined a French Marxist organization.[6]

In 1946, Jumblatt helped establish the "National Liberation Bloc," a political group in which a distinguished group of professionals and intellectuals debated political and ideological issues. The bloc, which soon boasted about seventy-five members, included former president Alfred Nakash (1941-1943); Abd al-Hamid Karami, mufti, notable and father of the late premier Rashid Karami; and Abdallah al-Aleily, a Sunni sheikh and distinguished linguist; Umar Beihem, a Sunni notable; Jawad and Fouad Boulus; and others.[7] In an interview, Al-Aleily suggested that the seeds of the Socialist Party were planted in the Liberation Bloc. The bloc's meetings revealed common ideological ground between some members, such as George Hanna, Jumblatt, and Fouad Rizk, that led to close contact between them. During these meetings, Al-Aleily discussed with Jumblatt the possibility of founding a party, while preserving the Lebanese National Movement as an electoral platform.[8] Jumblatt then called for a meeting in his house in Beirut to discuss the idea. The meeting was attended by Albert Adeeb, Fareed Jubran, Abdallah al-Aleily, Fouad Rizk, and George Hanna.[9] Most of them were either friends from college years or were associated with the inner core group, namely with Jumblatt and al-Aleily. Shortly thereafter, on May 1, 1949, the party was officially established. (See table 3.1).

Despite Sitt Nazira's objections to the idea of her son establishing a socialist party, Jumblatt thought it could carry him to national politics by transcending his narrow Druze traditional base of support.[10] Certainly the PSP in its early years touched an important chord in Lebanon's body politics, which was reflected in its widespread support from the rural poor population and leftist intellectuals.

The PSP was designed to be a mass popular political party with a secular socialist ideology, largely influenced by European socialist parties. The multisectarian composition of its leadership since its inception suggests the party commitment to secularism—that is, the total separation of the church from the state. But the party failed to build a multisectarian national organization despite its leaders. Why did it fail? Was it because of the multisectarian composition and the structure of political power in Lebanon? Can the failure be attributed to political choices made by PSP leaders? Is it a combination of both, or could it be attributed to some other factors?

The PSP founders were composed of young middle-class professionals, mostly non-Maronite Christians united by a belief in secularism

Table 3.1.
PSP LEADERSHIP IN 1949

NAME	RELIGION	PLACE & DATE OF BIRTH	PROFESSION	CLASS ORIGIN
Kamal Jumblatt	Druze	Moukhtara, 1917	Lawyer	Feudal
Abdullah Al-Aleily	Sunni	Beirut,1914	Sheik/Linguist	Upper Middle
Fouad Rizk	Greek Catholic	Mashghara, 1900	Lawyer	Upper Middle
Albert Adeeb	Maronite	Mexico,1908	Publisher	Middle
George Hanna	Christian Orthodox	Shweifat, N.A.	Physician	Lower Middle
Fareed Jubran	Catholic	Cyprus, 1912	Accountant	Lower Middle

Source: Abdallah al-Aleily, PSP founding member, interview by author, Beirut, July 1987.

punctuated by socialist ideas. At least one of the founding members openly professed his belief in Marxism.[11] This core group, as Fareed Jubran contended in an interview, also possessed a common vision regarding the unjust social and political system in Lebanon. More important, the class and religious/sect composition of the founding group also reflects their personal interests in building a secular socialist party.[12]

The presence of Maronite and other Christians within the PSP leadership, members of the dominant status groups in Lebanon, suggests that at least initially, the status system of domination in Lebanon did not have any bearing on the members' decision to join the PSP. Jumblatt had difficulty in attracting a group of Christian intellectuals, including Maronites, to his party. Paradoxically, the Sunni and Shiite sects were underrepresented among the leaders. Perhaps this was sheer coincidence, as Jumblatt had met a number of those who later became party members during his education in missionary schools, and later at the St. Joseph University in Beirut. In fact, two of Jumblatt's friends at the Institute of Aintura, a French missionary school, Fouad Rizk and Emille Tarabaye, became members of the leadership council shortly after the PSP was established in 1949.

The homogeneity of the founding group members is worth noting; three of the five were lawyers; one was an accountant; and one was a linguist. The five all resided in the capital, Beirut, and shared similar class origins (with the exception of Jumblatt who was of feudal class origins) and educational backgrounds. This suggests that the members' "class situation" may have had some weight in their decision to become party members.[13] Most had political aspirations and believed that the party might carry them to political position within the state apparatus. In fact, many of them became members of cabinets and parliaments or occupied high-ranking positions in the state's bureaucracy.

As a PSP leader, Kamal Jumblatt, one of the main political leaders of the Druze and presumably a pillar of the political establishment, placed the party in a unique position in the country's body politics. The PSP was an opposition and leftist secular party, yet due to Jumblatt's status in the power structure), the party was drawn into the consociational political arrangement.[14] Such characteristics of the party attracted many young and ambitious professionals. The committee framed the political principles of the party. Other contributors, such as Saeed Himadeh and Joseph Hajjar, helped lay down the economic principles; Fouad Bistani and Majid Fakhri contributed to the philosophical and cultural bases; Al-Aleily drafted the party's principles and some segments of the introduction.[15] The party constitution was drafted by Fouad Rizk. Al-Aleily notes that Jumblatt would have preferred to forgo a written constitution, based on his favorable impression of the British model of government.[16] The political principles of the group were called *al-Mithak,* or the pact; the very use of the term "pact" is significant. It implies a political contrast with the National Pact of 1943. While the latter was based on sectarian divisions between the political elite of the different sects, the PSP promoted the principles of secularism and democratic practice. By establishing the PSP, Jumblatt attempted to transcend his narrow role as a Druze leader and started to navigate against the ideological and social currents of sectopolitics. This task, as the decades to follow have proven was a formidable one.

To a great extent, the homogeneity of the inner core group in terms of class background, education, profession, and ideological orientation saved the leadership from factionalism. This homogeneity contrasted sharply with the heterogeneity of the Lebanese society the PSP leaders wished to lead. In a manner, the social perspectives of the PSP elite were radically different from that, say, of a Shouf Druze peasant, urban working-class Shiite, or an under-class Maronite in Kisirwan. The PSP task was to bridge the gap between its secular socialist goals and the public, which was sharply divided along sectarian lines.

JUMBLATT-CHAMOUN RELATIONS: FROM ALLIANCE TO CONFRONTATION AND THE LEADERSHIP COMPOSITION

The party witnessed its golden age during the period from 1949 to 1953 period. The PSP multisectarian leadership enhanced the party's secular credentials, and the party appealed to the Christian and Muslim masses alike. PSP officials attributed the party's relative success to the political decisions made during that period. According to leadership council member Fouad Salman, the short-lived alliance of Kamal Jumblatt with Camille Chamoun in the Socialist National Front (1951-1953) created a political base that was capable of neutralizing (at least temporarily) the effects of sectopolitics on the party. This is particularly true when one considers that the alliance included key Muslim and Maronite figures, such as Camille Chamoun (Maronite), Emille Bustani (Maronite), Elie Mukarzil (Maronite), Anwar al-Khateeb (Sunni), Ghassan Tweni (Greek Orthodox), and Butrus Edde (Maronite), all of whom were mobilized against the corrupt presidency of Bishara al-Khoury.[17] During this period, Kamal Jumblatt was elected as secretary-general of the Socialist National Front. According to Shaker Shaiban (leadership council, 1950), this political alignment with Chamoun in the period from 1949 to 1953 allowed the PSP to navigate with relative ease in Lebanon's turbulent sea of sectopolitics.[18]

CHAMOUN RENEGED ON HIS REFORM PLANS, GENESIS OF 1958 CRISIS

Camille Chamoun, a member of the Socialist Front, won the presidential election of 1952. Soon after he reached the presidency, he reneged on the reform program that he promised his party would accomplish. He also started courting Western powers and expressed interests in joining the Baghdad Pact, which outraged the opposition, led by Kamal Jumblatt and other Muslim leaders.[19] In effect, Chamoun's unwillingness to reform the political system and his drive to join the Western alliance led to an intense political schism within the ruling class, which became largely divided along sectarian lines. Chamoun rallied the support of key Maronite bosses and the Muslim community closed ranks under the leadership of Saeb Salam, Rashid Karami, Sabri Hamadeh, and Kamal Jumblatt.

The PSP leaders decided to embark on a policy of opposition to Chamoun, in particular his support of the Baghdad Pact and later his support of the Eisenhower Doctrine. According to the PSP officials interviewed, the leaders took their time to design a policy that responded to Chamoun's foreign and domestic policies. Moreover, they revealed that Jumblatt was the primary person to articulate that policy; his views received the endorsement of the leadership council without any significant change or opposition.[20] The PSP leadership and Muslims in general viewed Chamoun's policies as a direct violation of the spirit of the National Pact, which professed the neutrality of Lebanon.[21]

THE EMERGENCE OF ARAB NATIONALISM AND DISSENTION IN THE PSP CADRE: THE BUILD-UP OF THE 1958 CRISIS

The 1958 crisis coincided with the intensification of the Cold War between the United States and the Soviet Union in the Middle East. A related factor that also came into play was the rising tide of Arab nationalism in the region spearheaded by Gamal Abd al Nasser of Egypt. Arab nationalism was on the rise particularly after the 1956 tripartite war (France, Britain, and Israel) against Egypt in reaction to Egypt's nationalization of the British company that operated the Suez Canal. Chamoun adamantly refused to bend to the Muslims' demand to sever diplomatic ties with France and Britain after their attack on Egypt. Instead, he opted to increase his links with the Western alliance.

This situation was aggravated by Chamoun's insistence on amending the constitution so he could run for a second term and by the gerrymandering of electoral districts to eliminate some of his political opponents. The full-blown crisis came in 1957 after a large group of prominent leaders (such Saeb Salam and Kamal Jumblatt) were defeated in the parliamentary elections. This event secured for President Chamoun the two-thirds majority he needed to amend the constitution. The opposition charged that the election was rigged and called for Chamoun's removal.[22]

The debates within the PSP leadership mirrored the political discourse in the country, which was centered on developing a coherent policy to deal with political reform and the emergence of Arab nationalism at the regional level. The first outcome of this debate was the surfacing of dissenting voices who called for a full endorsement of an Arab nationalist program that supported Egyptian-Syrian unity (1958-1961). The protagonists of this movement were Clovis Maksoud (his uncle is George Hanna, a PSP founding member) and Mouris Sakr, both Christian, who were advising members (in the second echelons) of the party.[23]

Jumblatt and the majority of the leadership council believed that Nasser was going too fast in his anti-West policies and particularly in his nationalization of the Suez Canal. Maksoud said that such tactical differences between the PSP and Nasser were predicated by the party's position on Arab unity and Arab nationalism in general.[24] Jumblatt did not adhere to Arab unity in the form presented by Nasser; he felt such unity could be achieved gradually in some way.[25] For him, the European Economic Community was a living model that the Arabs could emulate. Maksoud and Sakr did not accept this view, and they were expelled from the PSP. Their expulsion did not create a major schism in the party because Jumblatt gained an overwhelming majority within the leadership.[26]

This did not mean that Maksoud and Saker's views were not supported within the lower ranks of the party hierarchy. In an interview, Sleiman Basha (Druze from Beirut, working-class background), stated that after the Suez Canal crisis (1956), the party held a meeting of its general assembly during which two main views were expressed: those in support of Nasser's policies and those that were opposed. Basha claimed that "the leaders of the conservative anti-Nasser faction were those professionals and opportunists who saw no benefit in antagonizing the Chamoun regime, and thus undercutting their bids for public office."[27] So it happened that the majority of those anti-Nasserites were Christians—more precisely, Maronites. Basha maintained that there were strong Arab Nationalist tendencies at the rank-and-file level of the general assembly. According to Basha, the views aired in the PSP assembly largely reflected the political and class interests of the individuals espousing them. The political aspirants, the party professionals, were conservatives and favored a policy of accommodation with Chamoun. People like him, of lower-class origins, agreed strongly with Nasser's message of social change and revolution.[28]

As the events of 1958 unfolded,[29] the anti-Nasser faction within the party refused to take part in the military insurrection; thus the schism within the PSP was crystallized. That faction was led by Fadallah Talhouk[30] (the only Druze) and Ilie Mukarzel (Maronite, PSP parliamentary candidate 1957), both advising members in the PSP hierarchy. Most of their followers were Maronites.[31] The anti-Nasser faction favored disengagement from pro-Nasser policies and called for the party to distance itself from the quagmire of Arab nationalism. They advocated a "Lebanonist" line that was very different from the party's position.[32]

ARAB NATIONALISM AND THE SYSTEM OF DOMINATION: THE CHRISTIANS' PERCEPTIONS

To understand the position of the dissenting anti-Nasser members, one has to examine their perceptions of Arab nationalism. For some Christians, pan-Arabism was synonymous with Islam, and thus could threaten the Christians of Lebanon. The unity between Syria and Egypt raised their anxieties and fears. This thinking was prevalent at the time within the Christian Maronite community and was made more so by the political campaign launched by President Chamoun and his allies to discredit the opposition. It is quite compelling to realize that the neutral political position of the Maronite patriarch, al Moushi, and a number of other Maronite leaders did not succeed in defusing the sectarian polarization in the country.

Why were members of a presumably secular political party like the PSP affected by sectopolitics? I put this question to a number of PSP officials, who responded unanimously that most of these "comrades" were new in the party and thus not well grounded in PSP ideology and political orientation. This factor, according to the interviewees, could explain the defection of Maronite members after the Jumblatt-Chamoun alliance was dissolved.[33]

However, it is crucial to mention that Arab nationalism and the increasing potential of Arab unity was not solely a "Muslim thing" but carried with it a threat to the system of domination in the country whereby the Maronite political elite and bourgeoisie were the main benefactors. The dominant social group viewed Arab nationalism, which was packaged with calls for social reforms, as a threat to its class and status interests. As M. S. Agawani noted, large numbers of Christian Maronites saw Arab nationalism as a threat to the independence of Lebanon and to their prominent role in government and society.[34] Agawani argues that the Christians' age-old fear of being submerged in a predominantly Muslim Arab world was reinforced considerably after Nasser's revolution.[35]

I agree that the Maronite political elite represented by Chamoun and supported by other Christians and a minority of Muslims feared losing their political hegemony in Lebanon's power structure. They perceived Arab nationalism as a political force that could undermine the system of domination in which they occupied a favorable position vis-à-vis the Muslims and other non- Maronite Christians.

The anti-Nasser dissenting members of the PSP leadership were the rank of advising members, mostly professionals (particularly lawyers), and predominantly Christian Maronites. This observation supports my contention that the "structure of power," although mediated by a political variable—in this case the emergence of Arab nationalism—influenced the distribution of the political forces within the party.

In hindsight, all Lebanese political parties that may be perceived as a threat to the system of domination were destined to acquire a sectarian character due to the sectarian constitution of the dominant group. The dominant position of the Christians, particularly the Maronites, in the class and status structures helped to condition the political struggle in Lebanon. Most members of the dominant status groups seemed influenced by sectopolitics and thus tended to side with the dominant political force within their sect. This fact is revealed in the weak support that all leftist political groups in Lebanon received from the Maronite community.[36] In a reflection on the 1958 experience, Jumblatt wrote: "the PSP leadership was slow in drawing crucial lessons when hundreds of partisans and thousands of PSP supporters in the Christian areas such as Kisirwan [a predominantly Maronite area] withdrew from the party as result of our opposition of Chamoun." He concluded that "Christians in general see the Maronite President of the Republic as their paramount leader, thus the majority of Christians have an unsettled feeling when they oppose him. Even when this opposition is for the sake of fulfilling a national program that could benefit all."[37] Jumblatt wrote these lines 25 years after the party's establishment.

Jumblatt's observation is not uncharacteristic of societies with aligned systems of domination with class and ethnic/religious components. Frank Parkin studied such systems of domination and wrote about the case of Catholics in Northern Ireland. He observed that the exclusionary closure (closed system) on the part of Protestant workers yields certain tangible advantages in the shape of an established monopoly of skilled and better-paid jobs as well as other material and symbolic prerequisites that flow from the control of political office. Parkin points out that the groups singled out for exclusion by the labor movement of the culturally dominant group are therefore those that already suffer marginal political status and whose own organizing and defensive capacities are seriously diminished. Individuals of the dominant group irrespective of their social class are tied with the entire system of domination and are the honorary members of the dominant status group, which provides them with a comparative advantage over the subordinate groups.[38]

In Lebanon, there is ample evidence to support that the Christians, particularly the Maronite sect that benefited from the system of domination, tended to support the political system.[39] Indeed, and as Parkin contends, the exclusion of Muslim, subordinate groups appears to occur by policies the dominant class/sect itself conducts via the state. Parkin adds that it is only through the action of the state that cultural groups become hierarchically ranked in a manner that enables one to effect closure against another. The Lebanese case provides strong evidence that social groups that benefited in material (better-paid jobs) and nonmaterial terms (such as prestige) were tied in with the system of domination and acted as defenders of the status, in effect defending the dominant social class and its political system.

These observations explain why the Christians and particularly the Maronite members defected from the PSP. Despite their defection, the leadership council itself remained committed to its Arab nationalist goals. This helped in maintaining common grounds which saved the leadership council from defection. The inner core of the party withstood the flow of sectopolitics and remained committed to Jumblatt's leadership.

THE 1958 CRISIS: PSP LEADERSHIP'S CHOICES AND ALTERNATIVES

In this section and in the following one, I explore the root causes of the democratic crisis and breakdown in Lebanon as informed by the PSP elite behavior during the years from 1958 and 1975. Five main contributing factors could explain the breakdown: The first is of a subjective nature that deals with the political choices made by the PSP elite. Those choices were influenced by personal ambitions and goals, political orientations and ideology. The second factor deals with the structural and political constraints that the PSP elite had to reckon with prior to and during the crises. This factor influenced the range of alternatives and incentives available to the leaders. The third factor is the absence of consensus over the rules of the political game between key elite members and the lack of mechanisms to regulate or mediate conflict. The fourth factor is the political dynamics of the crises that influenced the elites' courses of action. The fifth factor is the international and regional elements that came into play and contributed to certain political outcomes much beyond the local political elites' control.

Central to this inquiry is the question of why the PSP decided to participate in an armed insurrection that paralyzed the democratic process in 1958. In my interviews with a dozen PSP officials who were either in the leadership council or occupied other positions within the hierarchy then, there was a consensus that the party's participation in the revolt was a necessary evil. They contended that at that time Kamal Jumblatt and a number of party members lost their parliamentary seats to Chamoun's supporters, which aggravated already sour relations between the party and the Chamoun's government.

Moreover, they said that Jumblatt personally felt betrayed and cheated by Chamoun, who reneged on his personal commitments to Jumblatt's Socialist Front prior to his election in 1952.[40] There is an additional wrinkle to the story, and that is: Jumblatt and Chamoun were both leaders from the Shouf Mountains, a traditional (particularly since the nineteenth century) battleground between the Druze and Maronite feudal lords. This is something that both Shouf leaders inherited and carried in their caps and sleeves into modern Lebanon.[41]

Most important, however, I found that ten out of twelve interviewees placed priority on the fight against Chamoun and his foreign policy designs over maintaining the democratic process. The majority thought the insurrection was necessary to correct the wrongs done by Chamoun's regime. This finding shows a lack of commitment to democratic practices and rules on part of the PSP leaders. The leaders interviewed saw political participation in the democratic process and revolution as a continuum. In fact, none of the interviewees raised the issue of democracy. They all shared a common belief in the Clausewitzian dictum that says: "War is the continuation of politics by violent means."

The political behavior of the PSP during the 1953 to 1958 period cannot be explained without analyzing Jumblatt's own political thought. He viewed compromise and coexistence with opposing political forces as tactics within a strategy of revolutionary change.[42] According to Shaker Shaiban, prior to 1958, Jumblatt did not call for armed struggle as a means to assume power.[43] Shaiban added that Jumblatt was committed to a "democratic pluralistic socialism" option, and it was clear to those around him that he believed that this goal could be achieved by peaceful means.[44] Fareed Jubran, who was also in the leadership council during the crisis, maintains that the PSP reacted to Chamoun's policies and offensive to liquidate the party.[45] Fouad Salman, who was then the leader of the PSP's Beirut branch, presented a similar argument, saying that Chamoun and the Maronite elite reacted because Jumblatt was the first Druze leader who succeeded in building an alliance with the Arab national movement at the regional level and in forging closed links between the Druze, the Sunni, and Shiite communities at the local level. Accordingly, Salman added, the Maronite elite viewed the emergence of such Muslim-Arab alliance as a threat to its hegemonic status in Lebanon.[46] Chamoun was determined to curtail Jumblatt's growing influence before it was too late.

It is certain that prior to the crisis, the PSP was not considering the military option to change the regime. According to party officials, the PSP attempted to play by the rules of the political game, and its behavior prior to the crisis validates this view. Nonetheless, the party's behavior during the 1958 crisis demonstrated that its leaders were more concerned with how to change the power relationship in Lebanon—the structure and distribution of political power—than in maintaining the democratic process.[47] PSP officials argued that the fight against Chamoun's foreign policy was a "must" dictated by regional, international, and domestic considerations. These perceptions were further reinforced after Jumblatt lost his parliamentary seat to a Chamoun supporter and Chamoun moved to ban the PSP, coupled with the harassment to its supporters. Under such conditions the PSP was put on the defensive; the party then lashed out to recover lost ground.

The PSP officials believed that Chamoun's alliance with the West was designed, on the one hand, to strengthen the president's grip on power, and on the other, to safeguard the Maronite elite's dominant position within the power structure by offering Western powers a foothold in Lebanon under a Maronite political cover. Therefore, the PSP leaders' political choices were screened by the overriding concern with: denying Chamoun a short-term victory (reelection), and the longer term implications that this victory could bring to bear on the reinforcement of the political hegemony of the Maronite elite. These two considerations prevented PSP leaders from designing policies to sustain the democratic process. Particularly when Chamoun put the PSP and its allies on the defensive after the 1957 elections, policies were engineered on the basis of calculus of power under the pressures of the moment. This fact supports my thesis that structural elements, particularly power structures, not only shaped the menu of choices but helped to prioritize the political alternatives available to PSP leaders in 1958. The structure of power and state institutions provided the ground rules for a political dynamics (where actors' political choices affect outcomes) that could not be controlled by the democratic process. Political actors were sharply divided and deeply entrenched in their positions, which left little room for compromise and political maneuvering. Any meaningful political compromise entailed a change in the distribution of political power and resources, something that the dominant Maronite elite in Lebanon was not willing to give up without a fight. Juxtaposed to the dominant group's position was that of the subordinate social groups (Muslim elite), mobilized by a set of political elements (international, regional, and domestic), who could not settle for less than what they already had in terms of political power and resources. All the conflicting forces believed was that regional and international winds were blowing in their direction and could be utilized in the struggle for power and resources. Chamoun thought that the Western powers would defend his regime and thus enhance the Maronite political hegemony, and the opposition camp thought that Nasser and the Arab radical forces in alliance with the Soviet Union could alter the domestic correlation of forces in their favor.

Given the structure of power, Chamoun's attempt to undermine the opposition set in motion a political dynamic fueled by the opposition's defense of its position. The PSP had to choose whether to be co-opted, and thus abandon its political line, or to fight to defend the party.

Therefore, political and social structures (distribution of power) provided the initial contextual condition, predispositions, the parameters for a political dynamic; outcomes were decided by actors' interactions and their respective choices at that given moment (such as the ones mentioned above). The failure of the democratic institutions to provide political actors with long term horizons that would allow them to think about the future rather than present outcomes exacerbated the conflict and reduced the possibilities for compromise.[48]

The PSP contributed to the crisis dynamics by participating in an armed insurrection to achieve its political objectives; it succeeded in organizing a national opposition that led to Chamoun's partial defeat. In hindsight, both parties were partially right in their assessments of the regional and international conditions. Chamoun did not succeed in gaining a second term, but he did succeed in maintaining the position of the Maronite elite in the power structure. The PSP and the Muslim political elite at large succeeded in introducing some adjustments in the distribution of power but not enough to tilt the balance in their favor. It is important to mention here that after the 1958 crisis, the political elite in Lebanon adopted the slogan: *"La ghaleb wa la maghloub,"* which means "No victors no vanquished." This slogan captured the power relations between the major contending forces, a relationship that rested at a new point of equilibrium, which at that time was satisfactory to the struggling forces. This equilibrium allowed the democratic process to resume after civil strife and an eight-month interruption.

THE PSP LEADERSHIP, 1960–1970: FROM REFORM TO RADICALISM

In the aftermath of the 1958 revolt and the sectarian polarization that accompanied it, the PSP leadership witnessed some important changes in class and religious composition. Such changes coincided with the radicalization of the PSP political line, an issue that merits some attention since it provides a window to look at how societal impulses and political dynamics succeeded in translating themselves into actual change in the makeup (religious and class) of the PSP leadership and in shifts in its political behavior.

When General Fouad Shihab became the president of the republic in 1958, his major task was to diffuse sectarian polarization. One of his major achievements was the 1959 Personnel Law, which included an affirmation of the constitutional requirement that Christians and Muslims should be equally represented in the state administration. Such a concession to the Muslim community was coupled with a shift in Lebanon's foreign policy toward President Nasser of Egypt. Moreover, the political elite, realizing the need to expand the regime's power base, increased the size of the parliament from sixty-six to ninety-nine seats, to provide wider representation.

At least initially, President Shihab's policies satisfied some of the key Muslim demands; thus the Muslim elite was persuaded to support his efforts. The Maronite political elite, on the other hand, emerged from the 1958 crisis shaken but not defeated. They succeeded in maintaining their hegemonic status at the helm of political power as the main dispenser of resources despite minor adjustments in power distribution (i.e., increasing number of Muslims in state bureaucracies).

During the 1960s, particularly after the collapse of the Egyptian-Syrian unity (1961), the element of Arab radicalism was diffused, at least momentarily, and consequently, tensions were relaxed. The early 1960s also brought a huge influx of Arab capital escaping nationalization from neighboring Arab states and an increase in the capital flow of petrodollars. These elements combined to lead to a period of tranquility and seeming prosperity.

General Shihab, the chief of the armed forces prior to his election, refused to support former President Chamoun's policies. Such a neutral stand made him an acceptable figure to the Muslim elite and the Muslim populace at large. In this spirit, Jumblatt and Shihab established personal friendship and rapport, which helped to speed up the rapprochement between the PSP and the new regime. In fact, during the Shihab regime the party participated in government and made serious efforts to introduce social and political reforms. Jumblatt, according to the informants and PSP officials I interviewed, thought that there was a good chance to reform the system from within and thus opted to play by the rules of the democratic game. This "honeymoon" between the PSP and the state lasted until the mid-1960s, when the hurdles of the regional Cold War caught Lebanon off guard again, particularly that the programs for social and political reforms which were sailing in the turbulent high seas of sectopolitics never saw the shore. By the end of President Shihab's term in 1964, the PSP optimism of the early years of the 1960s started to fade away.

By the mid-1960s, despite the macroindicators of economic prosperity (measured in terms of gross national product growth, foreign capital investments, and others), the crisis in income distribution and the lack of job opportunities reached dangerous proportions. This condition was best described by the widely cited report of the French International Institute for Research and Training for Standardized Development (IRFED) Commission that warned the Lebanese government of the miserable conditions of the peripheral areas of Lebanon, which were inhabited mainly by Muslims, particularly Shiite.[49] Furthermore, the acceleration of the capitalist transformation in the rural areas without social nets to cushion the process led tens of thousands of predominantly Muslim peasants and sharecroppers to be displaced and to suffer economic dislocation. This situation intensified the class struggle of the peasant class against large landowners and the agrobusinesses that encroached on their livelihood. From the mid-1960s up until the eve of the 1975 civil war, labor unions, peasant organizations, and the student movement formed a political bloc that polarized the country along class and political lines.

How did these general conditions play out within the PSP in terms of leadership composition or affect the nature of the political discourse within the party ranks?

The Leadership Council elected in 1960 was composed of four Druze; one Shiite; one Greek Orthodox; one Sunni; two Greek Catholic; and three Maronite. The number of Druze in this council was the highest since the PSP inception. According to the PSP officials I have interviewed, this jump in the number of Druze was not accidental. During and after 1958 crisis, the PSP responded to sectarian pressures and an increasing number of Druze joined the party, particularly during the crisis.[50] But the fact remains that the leadership council maintained its largely multisectarian composition. More important, during the 1960 parliamentary election, the PSP ran in elections in Beirut, Mount Lebanon, Biqa', and the South—it did not have any candidate in the North. Its candidates were also a multiconfessional group. In that election, the PSP presented eighteen candidates; twelve won seats, the largest ever in the party's history. The winners were distributed as followed: two Christians from Beirut; one Shiite from Baalbak; and two Druze, two Sunni, three Maronites and one Catholic from the Shouf, the main PSP stronghold.

Thus in 1960, the PSP managed to become the largest party bloc within the parliament. The Kataib Party, another major party in Lebanon, won six parliamentary seats. The PSP success reflected its increased visibility and political activism in most of Lebanon. But certainly the Shouf remained the stronghold of Jumblatt and his party. The election indicated also that the PSP was giving the democratic process a chance in an attempt to put forth its secular reformist platform. Consequently, the party participated in the Saeb Salam government of 1960 and occupied two cabinet portfolios. Jumblatt became the minister of education, and the PSP vice president, Nasseem Majdalani became minister of justice and the vice premier.

The PSP played by the rules of the democratic game until Shihab's reforms stalled and began to falter under his successor and follower, President Charles Helou (1964-1970). Then the PSP reembarked on a course of political opposition. Party officials reflecting on that period stated that Jumblatt participated eagerly in the Shihab government with a political reform program that the PSP hoped to implement.[51] By 1964 Jumblatt started realizing that reforming the political system, particularly secularizing it and undercutting the influence of big capital in the political process, was becoming harder to achieve. Again, confronted by institutional resistance, particularly the intransigent position of the Maronite elite toward reform, Jumblatt and his party started developing radical ideas for social change. While he participated in power, Jumblatt realized the difficulty of reforming from within. The administrative changes he introduced in his ministry of education remained limited and without any far-reaching effect on the modernization and rationalization of the state bureaucracies. Corruption, nepotism, and clientelism against the backdrop of sectarian quotas had diminished the chances of establishing a system based on meritocracy and secular values. Perhaps these years of "positive engagement" with the state were critical in shaping Jumblatt's radical political thinking, which influenced his future political behavior toward the state and the consociational democratic system. His frustration with the political system was expressed one year after his participation in the government of Saeb Salam in 1961, when he wrote: "Lebanon's capitalists exploit brutally and shamefully the masses in association with some religions feudal lords who participate in this process of oppression and extortion of the masses . . . those that possess lands, institutions, and real estates valued at the tens of millions." Jumblatt adds that "the forces of reaction continue to exploit the sectarian sentiments of the people in an attempt to divert the people's attention from pursuing their socialist objectives in social change."[52]

CHANGES IN THE PSP LEADERSHIP IN THE 1960S

The social-class composition of the PSP leadership also underwent significant alterations in the 1960s. Some of the new leaders came from rural lower-middle-class families, and were graduates of public schools, such as the Lebanese University. (See table 3.2). This is in sharp contrast with the leadership during the 1950s. As mentioned earlier, the PSP constituted a political magnet for those middle-class professionals who were politically ambitious, particularly in the first two decades of the party's history. In contrast, during the 1960s and early 1970s[53] an increasing number of lower-class people joined the PSP, awakened by the sobering realities of the lack of employment opportunities (unemployment amounted about 12 percent of the workforce in 1970)[54] and the increasing gulf between the poor and the rich.[55] All of these factors were exacerbated by an intensification in the Arab-Israeli conflict, which brought into Lebanon a new actor: the Palestinian resistance.

Again, the PSP had to ponder these new conditions and their ramifications on Lebanon's political life. In the early 1960s, Shakib Jaber (middle-class Druze from Aley) and Abbas Khalaf (middle-class Greek Orthodox from Souk al-Gharb, Mount Lebanon) advocated an Arab National line within the PSP, but these leaders were not expelled from the party as Maksoud and Saker had been. According to PSP officials, the reasons why they remained within party ranks was due to two main factors: Jumblatt's realization that the movement of Arab nationalism,

Table 3.2.
THE PSP LEADERSHIP IN 1964

NAME	RELIGION	PROFESSION	CLASS ORIGIN
Kamal Jumblatt	Druze	Lawyer	Feudal
Salim Kuzah	Maronite	Lawyer	Middle
Muhsin Dalloul	Shiite	School Teacher	Middle
Fouad Salman	Druze	School Teacher	Lower Middle
Fareed Jubran	Christian	Accountant	Lower Middle
Abbas Khalaf	Christian Orthodox	Lawyer	Middle
Shaker Shaiban	Maronite	Lawyer	Middle

Source: Shaker Shaiban, a member of the leadership council, interview with author, Beirut, July 1987.

which was growing in the 1960s despite the failure of the Egyptian-Syrian unity, was progressive in nature and could help in creating a new social order in the Arab world. The second reason was that the protagonists, Jaber and Khalaf, did not want to face Jumblatt head on, and thus were more flexible in their approach than Maksoud and Saker had been. But, nonetheless, the fact remains that Jumblatt perceived the regional and international conditions in the 1960s differently after his radicalization by his experiences in the period from 1958 to 1964. In particular, he had developed a keen awareness of the revolutionary experiences of Vietnam, Cuba, and Algeria, the radical regimes that came to power in Iraq, Sudan, Syria, South Yemen, and elsewhere. Jumblatt's universe, henceforth, was constructed around the images of the revolutions occurring around him and the aura of idealism that they spread worldwide.[56] Moreover, his frustrations with the political process made Jumblatt more susceptible to a revolutionary course of action than to a democratic evolutionary one.[57] I think this is critical for our understanding of the political choices that predicated PSP behavior in the 1970s.

ARAB NATIONALISM REVISITED AND THE PSP: THE PALESTINIAN FACTOR

By the late 1960s and early 1970s, the debate on Arab nationalism continued within the party, but now the presence of the Palestinian armed resistance in Lebanon moved the country into the center stage of the Arab-Israeli conflict, creating a new political reality in the Arab world and in Lebanon's body politics. Commitment to the Palestinian cause became tantamount to the commitment to Arab nationalism, as the former was central to the latter. During that period an increasing number of PSP leaders came in direct contact with the leaders of the Palestinian Liberation Organization (PLO) operating from Beirut.[58] Consequently, the PSP amended its political program by accepting the principle of Arab nationhood and calling for the formation of a Democratic Confederation of Arab States. The PSP even amended its party slogan, "Free citizens and happy people," to "Freedom, Socialism and Arabism."

These changes in the PSP program reflected a change in the balance of power within the leadership in favor of the "Arabist" wing. It is important to mention here that the changes in the PSP's political program and composition came at a time when the increased activism of leftist political groups, labor unions, peasant organizations, and the student movement created a mood of radical social and political change. In the 1960s this mood in Beirut was in tune with international radicalism that reverberated in most parts of the world.

Social movements confronted a regime that failed to deliver any meaningful social reform or to provide basic services to rural areas when rampant poverty and increasing levels of social inequality reached critical levels. And above all, the system was unable to accommodate the rising expectations of the middle class and to satisfy their demands to open up the political process. The rising demands of new social groups strained the 1943 sectarian power-sharing arrangement between Muslims and Christians.

It is a typical case in which modernization created new social groups, particularly a middle class seeking wider political participation.[59] The middle class, particularly the Muslims, confronted an inflexible power-sharing formula that failed to respond to its needs and expectations due to the intransigent position of the dominant Maronite elite.[60] Neither the political system nor its inflexible sectarian structure of power distribution could cope with popular mobilization. The mobilized groups strained the consociational system because their satisfaction required an adjustment in the distribution of political power and economic resources. This necessitated a change of heart among the Maronite elite, who vehemently opposed the idea of change .

The Maronite elite was uncompromising, an attitude apparent with the formation of the so-called *"Helf al thulathy,"* the tripartite alliance between the three most prominent leaders of the Maronite, Pierre Jumayyel, Camille Chamoun, and Reymond Edde. The "helf" was formed in 1968 as a political response to the growing challenge that the leftist-PLO alliance was constituting. In this connection it is important to mention that during that period, extreme right paramilitary groups also emerged within the Maronite community, groups such as the Cedars' Guards, Al Tanzeem, the Maronite League, and others. These developments in the Maronite elite made the possibility of negotiating reform remote. Paradoxically, these developments also constrained the evolving liberal faction within the Kataib Party, which was more open to reform and dialogue with the left and the PLO.[61] As a result the Kataib gravitated toward the antireform camp, ostensibly to defend the Christians' privileges against the menace posed by the PLO and its Lebanese allies. The Kataib's shift to the right was motivated principally by the party's concern with maintaining its hegemonic status within the Maronite community—as the Christian representative par excellence—but particularly because ultra-right groups initially gained some political ground at the expense of the Kataib with their fiery rhetoric against Muslims, Palestinians, and leftist political parties.[62]

All these developments were taking place against a backdrop of escalation in the Arab-Israeli conflict that had a far-reaching effect on the delicate political balance on which the future of the political system hinged.[63] Regime supporters and opponents, alarmed and insecure about the spillover effects of the Arab-Israeli conflict, started reviewing their political options and priorities. A case in point was the radicalization of the PSP, which started to swing toward constructing a Leftist National Opposition Front. Parties on the right started forging relations with conservative Arab regimes and Israel.

During the 1950s, the PSP picked its allies from within the notables and intellectuals close to the political establishment. In contrast, since 1965 the PSP had been instrumental in building an alliance between the Lebanese Communist Party, the different factions of the Baath Party, the Arab National Movement, the Organization of Communist Work, the Nasserite Movement, and a host of independent leftist intellectuals. The PSP headed the alliance, and Jumblatt was elected as its nominal president until 1975, when he was elected officially by the

Central Committee of the leftist alliance, a position that he kept until his death in March 1977.

THE PSP'S LEADERSHIP BETWEEN REFORM AND REVOLUTION: THE BREAKDOWN OF THE CONSOCIATIONAL REGIME IN 1975

In the final analysis we need to know what Arturo Valenzuela describes as the range that exists for human choice. In his book *The Breakdown of Democratic Regimes: Chile,* Valenzuela raises the important question: To what extent are the actors in the human drama destined to live out their fate, or to what extent can they choose a different course?[64] In order to understand the political dynamics of the 1975 crisis, I reconstruct the political conditions in the few years that preceded it. My historical reconstruction is based on the accounts provided by political actors who were either personally involved in or well informed regarding the party's elite decisions. It is supplemented by other pertinent primary and secondary sources.

One of the interesting findings of this historical review is the role played by Kamal Jumblatt himself. Paradoxically, Jumblatt, although strongly opposed to the rules of the political game which perpetuated the Maronite elite hegemony, had acted as a moderating force for most of his political career. This was illustrated on several occasions, particularly when he thought that reform could be achieved within the system's democratic framework. An example is when the PSP embarked on its opposition movement against Bishara al-Khoury's regime in the late 1940s. At that time, perhaps, Jumblatt was not yet radicalized and his mind was not yet set on a specific course for political change. A second example is the PSP policy during the Shihab regime when the party enthusiastically engaged in the political process. A third occasion was in 1969, when Jumblatt became minister of the interior in the wake of that year's military clashes between leftist Lebanese and their Palestinian allies on one hand and the police forces and the regime supporters, the political right, on the other. After that time, Jumblatt acted as a moderating force and helped to defuse the volatile situation between the extreme forces of the right and the left.[65] However, his moderate voice became dimmer as social crises at home increased and the Arab-Israeli conflict at the regional level intensified.

By the early 1970s, the PSP became the backbone of the leftist alliance and Jumblatt emerged as the symbol of the progressive opposition and its main political leader. He was instrumental in drafting the 1975 political reform program, which was called *Al-Birnamaj Al-Marhali lilislah,* (the Interim Reform Program of the Lebanese National Movement [LNM]). The program was, in effect, a call to reform the political system, particularly by abolishing the sectarian system of political representation. Although the program was declared a few months after the 1975 civil war began, it did not call for revolutionary action.[66] Rather, it was a call to reform the political system by democratic peaceful means. The PSP, the Communist Party, the Organization of Communist Work, and other leftist groups did not totally give up their hope for the possibility of reform without launching a revolutionary war.[67]

In 1975 the PSP and the leftist alliance were not ready for a military confrontation with the regime and its rightist backers, yet they were dragged into it on terms that were decided elsewhere.[68] This view was expressed by most of the PSP officials, informants from the Communist Party,[69] and independents, such as Fuad Shbaklou,[70] a member of the LNM's central council. In interviews or in their writings, these officials expressed a view that the LNM under Kamal Jumblatt was against initiating a civil war. Jumblatt felt that public political consciousness had not yet evolved into a secular progressive one, especially within the Maronite community, which constituted about 20 percent of the population. Jumblatt and the LNM believed that a premature confrontation with the regime and the rightist militias could polarize the polity along sectarian lines, a development that could undermine the movement's secular reformist program.[71] This is yet another example where the sectarian social structure constrained the PSP's behavior.

In 1974, few months before hostilities began, Jumblatt candidly expressed his position vis-à-vis Lebanon's parliamentary democracy. He said that:

> "the parliament serves the PSP as a political platform [for airing the party's political views], and provides the PSP with political immunity. . . . The parliament is the place where the PSP can

> exert some pressure [on the political establishment] which could help the party in attaining some measure of national political liberties . . . the Parliament could provide the PSP some political gains that could serve its long term goals. . . . If the PSP acting in the same way as its allies were to sever its participation in the political process, this negative behavior could intensify the sectarian divisions in the society; in turn this could undermine the PSP efforts to organize the masses and increase the pressure on the ruling class.[72]

In a sense, Jumblatt viewed his participation in the political process as part and parcel of organizing a popular critical mass that was capable of introducing meaningful political change.[73] At the same time, he emphasized that Lebanon's sociopolitical conditions were not ripe for an armed struggle.

What happened to Jumblatt between the interview in December 1974 and April 1975 when hostilities broke out? Why was there a shift in the PSP's position? And what was behind this change?

To answer these questions, it must be kept in mind that Jumblatt did not reject outright or in principle the military option as a means to assume political power. He had adopted the military course once before in 1958, when his party promoted the avenue of armed insurrection against the President Chamoun's regime. But those interviewed for this study are certain that the PSP in 1975 was neither ready for a military campaign nor preparing for one in order to assume political power.

In my interviews with PSP officials and independent informants, all argued that Jumblatt was against the arming of the PSP members and against a general military training until well after April 1975. Prior to 1975 military training was very limited.[74] This fact suggests that Jumblatt was not yet committed to a violent overthrow of the government. He believed that the heterogeneity of Lebanese society and the mode in which political power is structured along sectarian lines, make PSP participation in the political process essential in order to present to the populace a new political vision, one based on secular and progressive principles. Jumblatt thought that most of the Muslim population sided with what he called "the Arab national line" while only to 30 to 40 percent of the Christians sided with it. Therefore, according to Jumblatt, he had to participate in the political process to persuade the Christians to side with him.[75] When the crisis began, Jumblatt stepped up his political campaign against the Kataib Party, the backbone of the Maronite elite and a staunch supporter of the system, and called for the party to be politically isolated. His effort was designed to exert pressure on the Maronite establishment and provide a chance for moderate voices to surface within that community. But his calls were to no avail, and in retrospect they backfired by generating more support for the Kataib.[76]

Sectopolitics proved more resilient than Jumblatt contemplated.[77] The Maronite community closed ranks behind the Kataib and its allies on the Christian front. Nonetheless, from April to September 1975, Jumblatt viewed the crisis in political terms. That is, he continued to believe that a political settlement could be reached, but on the grounds of social and political reform based on the provisional reform plan of the LNM. Again, he misread the Maronite elite's position and perhaps underestimated the support it secured from Western quarters, mainly the United States, France, Israel, and later Syria, something that he later acknowledged.

From September to November 1975, Prime Minister Rashid Karami, a main figure in the Muslim elite, called for the formation of the National Dialogue Committee. The committee brought together the main representatives of the political elite to settle the crisis before it was too late. However, the committee could not even agree on an agenda for discussion and became engulfed in whether priority should be given to Lebanon's security and sovereignty (a euphemism for PLO political and military activity), or to political reform and power-sharing issues. The initial concerns were raised by the Maronite leaders, such as Pierre Jumayyel, president of the Kataib Party, Camille Chamoun, ex-president and also leader of the National Liberal Party, and Reymond Edde, leader of the National Bloc Party. The Muslim elite representatives, namely Saeb Salam, Rashid Karami, and Kamal Jumblatt raised the issue of power-sharing. The failure of the National Dialogue Committee was a clear indicator that the traditional rules of the political game revolving around a working consensus between the elite members had been lost. This meant in effect the collapse of the consociational arrangement.

The lack of an interelite consensus, compounded by the widespread popular mobilization, made the collapse of the system imminent. Exogenous factors, such as the alliances of the different members of the ruling elite with foreign actors, helped to polarize and divide the elite and contributed to their intransigent positions. In 1975, as was the case during the 1958 crisis (which largely had the same main protagonists), members of the elite were unable to work out their differences regarding the distribution of power from within. This, in my opinion, caused the main crack in the political system and made it vulnerable to strains emanating from other sources, both regional and international. As during the 1958 crisis, members of the elite tried to capitalize on regional and international changes in their fight for local power and resources.

Soon after the failure of the committee, the PSP started a major drive to arm and train its personnel. I believe that the committee meetings revealed to Jumblatt the futility of the situation and convinced him that the only avenue left was the battlefield. By early January 1976—-the war started in April 13, 1975 in Beirut—the PSP forces began participating actively in the war, particularly in the Damour-Jieh enclave, south of Beirut, dominated by forces loyal to Camille Chamoun's National Liberal Party. Jumblatt wrote that the real battle that would determine the future of Lebanon was to be fought in Mount Lebanon, the stronghold of the Christian militias; and so it happened that the majority of the Druze have also lived in Mount Lebanon for several centuries.[78]

Jumblatt initiated the Mountain War after the battle of Tal Azatar, the Palestinian refugee camp that fell to Christian rightist militia in August 1976. The main motive behind his decision was to break the military stalemate in Beirut by opening a new front to encircle the rightist militias and thus achieve a clear cut military victory.[79] In fact, the forces of the LNM and their Palestinian allies broke the backbone of rightist forces in the battles of the Upper Maten (in Mount Lebanon), which practically made the remaining military campaign a mopping-up operation. But soon the Syrian forces intervened to deny the leftist-PLO alliance an outright military victory, which could have entailed serious political ramifications at the regional level.

To sum up Jumblatt's choices: At first, he was hesitant to commit his party and leftist allies to a military adventure until the failure of the National Dialogue Committee. Thereafter, he chose what he believed to be an optimal course of action, deciding to initiate the Mountain War only when he believed that the LNM's objectives were within his grasp. Plausibly, this could have made Jumblatt the president of the new republic. Therefore, he acted in accordance with the rational-choice model by following a course of action that appeared an optimal one to him at the time. Of course, even Jumblatt acknowledged later that he was mistaken in his calculations. He misread the international and regional conditions, primarily the Syrian regime's intentions and goals in Lebanon which did not favor a LNM government.

Jumblatt was a player evolved in a game of mutual intransigence with his Maronite counterpart. He and the leftist coalition and a good segment of the Muslim elite thought that the PLO's military presence in Lebanon offered them a rare opportunity to extract significant political concessions from the Maronite ruling elite. Yet the Muslim-leftist alliance was confronted with an equally intransigent Maronite elite who had secured regional and international backing to hold its ground. In game theory parlance, a deadlock situation arose, where the actors involved believed that intransigence (a chicken noncooperation game) rather than compromise could achieve the most desirable outcome.[80] Such a deadlock brought the collapse of the consociational arrangement of 1943.

According to the consociational literature,[81] in societies that are organized in segments or pillars, followers are polarized, and elite should demonstrate accommodating behavior. Thus, when the elite, like its social power-base, becomes noncompromising in their behavior, they bring the consociational arrangement into crisis.[82] That was the situation of Jumblatt and his allies and their corresponding power-base during the 1975-1976 crisis. The political deadlock persisted until 1989, when the Lebanese elite finally signed on to a new consociational arrangement that gave Muslims an equitable share of power along the Maronite and Christian elite at large. This arrangement became known as the Taif Accord.

One last point worth mentioning here is that the PSP and the Kataib Party proved to be extremely crucial elements for the sustenance of the political system's stability, albeit the weakness of Lebanon's party system. Thus their failure to reach a compromise in 1975 led to the collapse of the consociational democracy, something perplexing in a presumably weak party system democracy.

The PSP leadership council of 1975 was elected shortly before the civil war. In terms of the social and sectarian distribution, it was no different from the 1960s. The significant change came much later, in the 1980s, when a new generation of PSP militia leaders started ascending the party echelon. (See table 3.3).

TABLE 3.3.
PSP LEADERSHIP 1975

NAME	PROFESSION	SOCIAL CLASS	SECT
Kamal Jumblatt	Lawyer	Feudal	Druze
Salim Kuzah	Lawyer	Middle Class	Maronite
Muhsin Daloul	School Teacher	Lower Middle	Shiite
Fouad Salman	School Teacher	Lower Middle	Druze
Bihjat Abu al-Hissen	Middle Ranking Employee	Middle Class	Druze
Riyadh Raad	Owner of Publishing House	Upper Middle	Shiite
Robeir Hanna	Lawyer-Businessman	Lower Middle	Christian Orthodox
Abdallah Shaya	Public Employee	Lower Middle	Maronite
Fareed Jubran	Lawyer	Middle Class	Christian Catholic
Tarek Shihab	Lawyer	Lower Middle	Sunni

Source: Joseph Kazi, PSP leadership council member, interview with author, Dair al-Kamar, Summer 1989.

THE PSP AFTER THE DEATH OF ITS FOUNDER AND THE ELECTION OF WALID JUMBLATT: "TRADITION" VERSUS "MODERNITY"

In March 1977, Kamal Jumblatt's life and political career were dramatically put to an end—he was assassinated by a few armed men who ambushed his car just a couple of miles from his home village, al-Moukhtara. His assassination was a serious blow to the Lebanese leftist movement from which it never recovered.[83]

His party also entered a new phase when his son, Walid Jumblatt, assumed the PSP presidency. While Walid Jumblatt was not a PSP leader, social pressures, particularly from the Druze followers of the Jumblatt clan, dictated his election. The process of succession illustrates vividly how sectopolitics, imposed itself on a presumably modern institution such as a political party.[84]

According to party members involved in the process of electing Walid Jumblatt that their choices were clear: Either elect another leader from among the leadership council and lose the traditional support base of the Druze, or they could elect a Jumblatt and preserve that base.[85] After lengthy deliberations, the leadership council caved in to the social and political pressures of a traditional society. Paradoxically, even secular parties, such as the Communist Party and the Organization of Communist Work, believed that Kamal Jumblatt's son Walid should succeed him.[86] This support was based on their belief that they could continue capitalizing on the PSP's Druze support base to serve the LNM secular project. This belief later was proven ill conceived; their support of Walid Jumblatt served sectopolitics instead.

The Druze, particularly the Jumblatt faction, reacted violently to Kamal Jumblatt's assassination. Traditionally, the son or the most revered person from the Jumblatt clan would succeed him. This tradition, inherited from the feudal times, is still observed among certain groups in Lebanon. For the Druze community, this tradition acquires more importance than is the case with other sects because the Druze do not have an independent clergy hierarchy; historically their religious leadership and officials have been appointed by the political chieftains. For over a century, the Jumblatt and Arislan feudal factions influenced clerical appointments, and that tradition continues to this day. In other Lebanese sects, the church or mosque is independent from political chieftains and enjoy relative freedom in engaging in intercommunal politics due to the existence of church/mosque hierarchy; the Druze do not have a formal clergy structure. The appointment of the highest Druze spiritual leader, *Sheikh al-Akl* (sheikh of the wisemen), is essentially a political appointment worked out between the Jumblatt and Arislan chieftains.[87] This fact partially explains why the Druze pay extra attention to their political leadership, the Jumblatt and Arislan factions, because they hold the power within the community. The Druze Jumblatt faction rallied behind Walid Jumblatt as they did for his father before him.

Ironically, Kamal Jumblatt's original intention behind the establishment of the PSP was to transcend the same power base that acted as a constraining social force even after his death. However, the strength of this tradition does not stem from its inherent inner power only; it also has been cultivated and reinforced by a political system based on sectarian political representation. Under such a system, sects feel compelled to abide and compete by the rules of sectarian representation in order to preserve their interests. Thus the Druze acted in accordance with the power arrangement that requires that they be represented by their traditional factions, namely the Jumblatt and Arislan clans. Obviously, the sectarian political representation and the social archaic traditions reinforce each other and provide the system with power to sustain and perpetuate itself.

Such a system inhibits the development of cross-sectarian parties because it is based solely on the political representation of sects. Perhaps this explains, why secular political parties in Lebanon enjoyed marginal political support while the PSP failed as a secular project in a hostile institutional and political environment.

THE PSP LEADERSHIP FROM 1978 TO 1998

The PSP leadership underwent significant changes during the period from 1978 to 1994, when the party was transformed into a war machine and most civilian posts in the party focused on the necessities of warfare. In the early 1980s, the PSP amended its internal structure by increasing the numbers of the rank of *Murshid* (advisor) from which the leadership council elects its members.[88] Advisors are the cadre of the party who constitute the leading activists, ideologues, organizers, and campaigners. The advisors were added to the leadership council, replacing it with a central committee and political bureau, adopting a Leninist party structure. Most of these new advisors were part of the military cadres that emerged after 1975 and Walid Jumblatt sought to provide them with leadership positions in an effort to consolidate the party's faltering discipline and the loss of the chain of commands when some militia leaders dared enough to challenge his leadership of the party.

The main characteristic of the party leadership during the years from 1978 to 1994 was its class composition. It was drawn largely (70 percent) from lower middle class and rural people, and had fewer professionals than the leaders of the earlier periods. The leaders also were younger than the proceeding ones—the average age of its members ranges between thirty and thirty-five years old, while the previous members of the defunct leadership councils averaged ages forty-five to fifty. In terms of the sectarian distribution of the members, about 65 percent were Druze; 15 percent Sunni (predominantly from Ekleem al-Kharoub and Biqa'), 10 percent Shiite (from Tyre and its environs); and 10 percent Christians (from the north: Koura and Tripoli). This contrasted with the makeup of the 1975 Leadership council.

In March 1994 the PSP reinstituted the leadership council and dissolved its central committee and the political bureau. The General Assembly of the party, attended by 631 delegates, approved. The sectarian distribution of the 1994 leadership council is as follows: six Druzes; three Maronites; one non-Maronite Christian; four Shiites; and three Sunnites. The leaders multiconfessional character is quite interesting, particularly because during his tenure, Walid Jumblatt concentrated on consolidating his Druze base more than on building a secular national organization. But apparently he is window-dressing his party to project a nonsectarian image, which could help enhance his national prestige.

The causes behind this last revision of the party's organizational structure is an expression of its internal crisis after 1989. Most members of the high echelons, militia commanders, lost their raison d'être and became inactive when the civil war ended. This inactivity increased the party's isolation even within the Druze community, especially when a number of these party's leaders were accused of being corrupt, receiving illegitimate kickbacks, and being involved in organized crime.

Finally in 1998, the PSP elected a new and expanded leadership council of 37 members in an attempt to widen the regional representation of areas that remained outside its reach since 1975. The significance of this expansion is a renewed commitment of the PSP to recuperate its national role. The council includes fourteen new members from regions such as Batroun, Kisirwan, and Tripoli. The first two are Christian districts that were under the hegemony of the rightist militias during the years of the civil war. It is also noticeable that the PSP is reinstituting its cadre school after a long absence. The school is to educate party members on socialist thought and Arab history. This measure indicates that the PSP is paying more attention to the importance of political education, particularly in an environment where sectopolitical ideology is the dominant one. The assembly also revealed a new interest of the PSP in reestablishing its links with the Lebanese Communist Party as well as other democratic forces after more than ten years of political isolation.

CHAPTER FOUR

The System of Domination and the PSP Rank and File, Class and Sectarian Composition, 1949–1994

STUDENTS OF LEBANESE POLITICS commonly believe that the PSP is a Druze party. Since its inception, however, the party has struggled to dispel such a notion. This chapter analyzes the data on PSP members recruited between 1949 and 1994. This analysis not only explains whether the PSP is or is not a Druze party, but more important, it examines the sociopolitical conditions under which the party recruited its membership and the factors influencing the recruitment process. Finally, the analysis presents patterns in the recruits personal profiles.

My main assumption is that the structure of power in Lebanon influenced the sectarian and class configuration of the PSP's rank-and-file membership. I examine whether the configuration of the PSP's rank and file influenced what Sartori termed "the way the party channels and expresses interests." If parties are important vehicles for representing social groups by channeling and expressing the interests of those groups, then it is imperative to define the social base of support of a given party.

This chapter is organized into six chronological phases, each of which depicts a main stage in PSP development. I present profiles of those individuals who joined the party during each of these phases. The data presented in this chapter was compiled by the author from PSP records.

An estimated 17,810 members were registered as PSP members between 1949 and 1990. Each member's record includes the date and place of birth, profession, and rank. I extrapolated the religion/sect of the members from the place of birth and surnames with the help of PSP book keepers.

The first phase (1949-1958) of this study discusses the popular appeal of the PSP since its foundation until the 1958 armed insurrection. The second phase (1959-1964) examines the impact events of 1958 on the class and sectarian configurations of members recruited later. These years were marked by close cooperation between the PSP and the regime of President Shihab; thus this phase is characterized by a shift in PSP policy from opposition to allegiance, a phase I have termed the years of constructive engagement.

During the third phase (1965-1970), PSP policy shifted to political opposition. During these five years, the PSP succeeded in leading an alliance that included the main parties of the left (Communist Party, Organization of Communist Work, Baath party, Syrian National party, pro-Nasser movements, and others). I explore the impact of PSP's shift on its popular appeal as reflected in the sectarian and class origins of members recruited during this phase.

The fourth phase (1971-1975) discusses the prelude to the civil war. This period is characterized by the rising socioeconomic crisis in the country punctuated by the military presence of the Palestine Liberation Organization (PLO). Here again I profile of those who joined the PSP under such conditions of crisis.

The fifth phase (1976-1977) is the civil war period I examine the impact of this crisis on the PSP's appeal to different social groups. The sixth phase (1978-1979), is the most difficult period in the party's history. It was marked by the assassination of the party leader. Of interest here is the change in party recruitment patterns under the leadership of Walid Jumblatt, the son of the founding father. Finally, this chapter concludes with a postscript about phase 7, 1980 to 1994.

PHASE I, 1949–1958: THE FOUNDATION OF THE PARTY

The first years after the party's establishment were its golden epoch. About 10,497 new members joined the party. Their origins and backgrounds

TABLE 4.1.

ESTIMATED CONFESSIONAL COMPOSITION OF THE LEBANESE POPULATION, 1984 (UNOFFICIAL) AND 1932 (LAST OFFICIAL CENSUS)

SECT	POPULATION 1984	% 1984	% 1932
Shiite	1,100,000	30.8	19.6
Sunni	750,000	21.0	22.4
Druze	200,000	5.6	6.8
TOTAL MUSLIMS	2,050,000	57.3	48.8
Maronites	900,000	25.2	28.8
Greek Orthodox	250,000	7.0	9.7
Greek Catholics	150,000	4.2	5.9
Armenian	175,000	4.9	3.9
Other Christians	50,000	1.4	1.6
Jews and others minorities	N.A.	N.A.	1.2
TOTAL CHRISTIANS	1,525,000	42.7	50.0
TOTAL	3,575,000	100.0	100.0

Source: Adapted from M. Johnson, *Class and Client In Beirut,* (London: Ithaca Press, 1986), p. 226.

were more diversified than those who joined the group after 1958. Druze members equaled 4,039 (40.38 percent) of the total; 2,319 (22.09 percent) were Christian; 2,127 (20.26 percent) were Shiite; and 1,812 (17.26 percent) were Sunni. Since its inception, the sectarian makeup of the PSP indicates the disproportionate representation of Druze, who according to an unofficial census in 1984, constituted less than 10 percent of the total Lebanese population. The Shiite, on the other hand, constituted about 30.8 percent of the total population; the Sunni, 22.4 percent; and, the Christians constituted 42.7 percent. (See table 4.1).

The representation of the Druze in the PSP sprang from the founder's reliance on the traditional power base of the Jumblatt family. Members of Druze families that supported the Jumblatt feudal faction since the eighteenth century (when the Jumblatt lords gained supremacy) became either supporters or members of the PSP. Their support for Jumblatt was based on communal feelings and allegiance. Most of Jumblatt's Druze supporters were of peasant origins; their families historically had worked on the lands of the Jumblatt feudal lords.[1] Thus their motivations to join or support the party were typical of a client-boss relationship.

TABLE 4.2.

PSP MEMBERSHIP DISTRIBUTION BY SECT: 1949–1958

YEAR	CHRISTIAN %	DRUZE %	SHIITE %	SUNNI %	MISSING CASES	TOTAL NUMBER
1949	56.33	38.61	0.31	4.75	2	318
1950	19.47	68.90	4.71	6.92	4	1,956
1951	15.90	74.48	6.10	3.52	3	1,053
1952	20.52	26.52	11.88	26.87	109	4,426
1953	24.81	34.36	20.07	20.76	27	1,756
1954	31.07	10.72	42.89	15.32	1	458
1955	20.16	22.58	53.76	3.49	5	377
1956	24.11	24.55	44.64	6.70	0	224
1957	10.00	78.75	1.25	10.00	1	0
1958	0.00	0.00	0.00	0.00	0	0

Source of data: PSP official records.

Jumblatt, aware of Lebanon's social and political structures and the limitations they imposed on intersectarian politics, gave special consideration to the role of sectopolitics when defining his political alliances. He argued that due to the power arrangement, Lebanese society is vertically divided along sectarian lines, rather than on class lines.[2] He believed that understanding sectopolitics was a key for comprehending the sociopolitical dynamics in the Lebanese body politics.

The PSP tested Jumblatt's abilities to bridge the contradictions between the PSP as a secular project and his traditional Druze power base. This is one of the main contradictions that the PSP as a political organization faces, a contradiction originating from Jumblatt's dual leadership of a Druze faction and a secular political group.

Nonetheless, PSP records show that when the party was founded in 1949, Christian members outnumbered all other sects. In that year about 178 Christians, 122 Druze, 1 Shiite, and 15 Sunni joined the PSP. (See table 4.2).

Most of these Christians and Druze were from al-Moukhtara, Kamal Jumblatt's own village, and its environs. Over 67 percent of the 1949 members were from Mount Lebanon.

From 1949 to 1957 the number of Christians who joined the party increased according to the same pattern as that of the Druze but at a lower ratio. Patterns of new-member recruitment from all sects clearly reveal the multisectarian nature of the party, especially during 1952.

In 1952 the PSP succeeded in recruiting members from most of the five administrative districts *(muhafazat)* in Lebanon. However, most of the new recruits (about 35 percent) were from Mount Lebanon, 33.24 percent from the Biqa', 13 percent from the district of Beirut, 12 percent from southern Lebanon, and 7 percent from the northern district of Lebanon.

As these data indicate, the PSP's main distribution areas were Mount Lebanon and the Biqa'. PSP leaders from the Biqa', such as Fuad Rizk, Shaker Shaiban, Shikrallah Nisrallah, and Fadlou Abou Haidar, were instrumental in recruiting PSP members from their areas. All of them assumed leadership positions in the 1950s.

Interestingly, all of them were Christian lawyers. In an interview with one party leader recruited in 1952, Mr. Mehsin Dalloul (a Shiite from the Biqa' and Defense Minister, 1992-) said that he was first contacted by Michelle Ghureib in the Zahle secondary school he attended. Ghureib was a Christian teacher who taught in the same school.[3] Dalloul became a member of the leadership council in 1975.

The director of the Zahle branch was Joseph Juraisaty, who left the PSP after 1958 and in the 1980s became director general of the president's office, a position equivalent to the White House chief of staff.[4] Recruitment in the Biqa' occurred primarily through PSP Christian cadres, especially those in Zahle, Mualeket Zahle, and their environs.[5] It is important to note that the Biqa' is predominantly Shiite. The Christian PSP cadres played a significant role in recruiting Shiite members between 1947 and 1957.

In southern Lebanon, where Shiites also constitute the overwhelming majority, the PSP attracted 526 members—11.88 percent of the total recruited in 1952. Several factors explain the upsurge in the number of PSP members in 1952, particularly within the Muslim communities. The first was the rising tide of Arab nationalism and Arab socialism in the region, with the Baath Party and the Nasserite movement (followers of Egypt's president Gamal Abd al-Nasser) representing the leading wave of that tide. Increasingly, the Shiite, Sunni, and Druze became the power base of most of the pan-Arab socialist parties.[6] The receptivity of the three

Muslim communities to socialist ideologies is attributed to their conditions of poverty and their resentment of the prevailing sociopolitical and economic order.[7] Thus Muslims, the socially, economically, and politically subordinate group, organized in anti–status quo political parties.

The second factor was Kamal Jumblatt's key role in the 1952 crisis, which brought the downfall of President Bishara al-Khoury's regime thus enhancing Jumblatt's party image and prestige (al-Khoury was the first president after independence; his presidency was characterized by corruption and nepotism). Jumblatt built an alliance with the different opposition figures in the country, creating the Socialist National Front in 1951. The front succeeded in staging a huge rally in August 1952 in the Shouf town of Dair al-Qamar. The rally was a show of force by the opposition, which included figures such as Maronite leader Camille Chamoun (who that same year won the presidential race as a Socialist Front candidate). Chamoun was a wealthy businessman from Dair al Qamar, a few miles away from Jumblatt's village. Thus regional and domestic factors contributed to the growth of the PSP as an organized political group.

Between 1949 and 1952 period sectopolitical polarization occupied a backseat, thanks to the short-lived Jumblatt-Chamoun alliance.[8] This explains why more Christians joined the PSP in that period than at any time since: 88.82 percent of the total PSP Christian membership joined in the first period, about 43 percent of them joining in 1952 (chi square = 1482.40, DF = 15, $p < 0.000$). The Christians represented 22.09 percent of the total party membership for the 1949-1957 period and were second only to the Druze (40.38 percent); the Shiite and the Sunni constituted 20.26 percent and 17.26 percent, respectively. The Druze, Shiite, and Sunni who joined the PSP between 1949 and 1957 accounted for 55.42 percent, 57.21 percent, and 63.31 percent of the total of each sect that joined until 1978.

In its early years, the PSP was also perceived by the Christians as a genuine Lebanese party with no clear pan-Arab orientation, a perception that contributed to increased Christian membership. However, some Christian Maronites such as Saeed Akel, a Lebanese poet and politician who during the 1975 civil war became a member of the rightist alliance, the Lebanese Front, and Raeef Abi Allmae', son of a prominent family, wanted more emphasis on the Lebanese character of the group and suggested adding the word "Lebanese" to the party name.[9] But Jumblatt and al-Aleily rejected the suggestion, turning from the notion of Lebanese nationhood or even Arabism and instead advocating a universal outlook to humankind seen from a socialist perspective.[10] This universal outlook attracted some intellectuals from different sects, particularly Christians who had been more exposed to the socialist thoughts emanating from France and its missionary schools in the Levant.

As was discussed in chapter 3, the issue of Arab unity became a major point of contention within PSP ranks. The outcome of the debate determined the party line on Arab nationalism and consequently influenced the sects of the new recruits. During the PSP's general assembly meeting held in 1956, discussions took place between those that supported Nasser's nationalization of the Suez Canal (which triggered the Tripartite War against Egypt) and those who thought that the move was a miscalculation and favored a position of neutrality in the conflict.[11] Sleiman al-Basha, who participated in the deliberations, said in an interview that some PSP members, particularly those who wanted to run for the parliament, suggested a tacit electoral agreement with Camille Chamoun.[12] Eventually this position was overruled and the PSP refused to make any agreements with Chamoun; this led to the defeat of PSP candidates (including Jumblatt) in the 1957 elections.

At this juncture some Christian professionals realized that the PSP was embarking on an opposition line that lessened their chances of attaining public office. The Chamoun crackdown against the PSP helped to reinforce that realization and also hindered recruitment attempts among all sects. PSP records illustrate very clearly the effects between 1952 and 1957. Data indicate that the new PSP recruits decreased from about 4,426 (1952) to about 1,758 in 1953, 567 in 1954, 372 in 1955, 224 in 1956, and less than 100 in 1957.

The 1958 revolt cut across class boundaries; poor Christians and Muslims fought each other along the dominant/subordinate status axis. The poor Muslims were revolting against their inferior status and the poor Christians defended their (perceived) superior status. The middle and upper classes were less affected by sectopolitics, although they led the masses in a conflicting course along sectarian lines. The loyalists consisted of the more conservative notables of Christian Mount Lebanon, as well as elements of the business, commerce, and finance bourgeoisie that had benefited from Chamoun's economic policies.[13] Some Muslim notables, such as Saeb Salam, Ahmad al-Assad, and

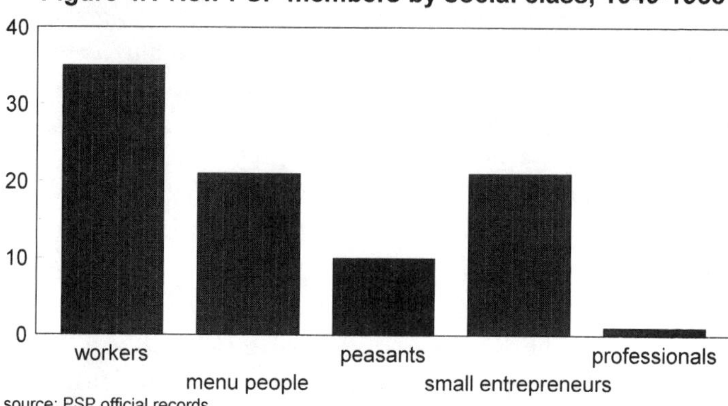

Rashid Karami, who belonged to the class of loyalists, joined the rebel forces because Chamoun sought to curtail their political influence.[14]

At one level Christians fought to defend their dominant status, and the Muslims fought to change their subordinate status. At another level the insurgent forces, although led by chieftains who could hardly be called progressive, were supported by young educated middle-class radicals.[15] Arab nationalists, the Baathists, a broad stratum of the professionals and intellectuals, the Communist Party, and others gave the insurgents a reformist character.[16] Thus conventional class or ethnic analysis does not provide a comprehensive explanation for the 1958 crisis.[17] It was an interelite conflict at one level, mostly divided along sectarian lines. On another level, the Muslim elite received the support of the Muslim poor. This can be seen in the social composition of the areas and districts that supported the insurgents.[18] These areas were the most impoverished in Lebanon.[19]

The PSP sectarian composition changed dramatically after the 1958 crisis, an issue discussed in the next section. Here we turn to the class composition of the PSP and the distribution of its members over Lebanon's five administrative districts *(muhafazat)* during phase 1. Between 1949 and 1957 the PSP attracted the poor masses. Workers constituted about 35 percent of the membership for this period and about 75 percent of all workers recruited between 1949 and 1978.[20] The second largest stratum, the menu people[21] (craftsmen, butchers, taxi drivers, shoe repairers, carpenters, and others) constituted about 21 percent of those recruited in phase 1 (1949-1957), and about 58 percent of all menu people recruited between 1949 and 1978. The workers, menu people, and the peasants (9.81 percent) comprised about 66 percent of PSP membership in its first phase, and about 41 percent of total party membership from 1949 to 1978. (See figure 4.1).

These above data indicate that in its first phase the PSP was primarily composed of workers and menu people. At this time the party was more diversified in its sectarian composition and attracted the impoverished masses. The peasant class constituted about 6.12 percent of all PSP recruits and 10 percent of those who joined during phase 1. Again, the vast majority (88 percent) of peasant members joined during the party's first years. The small entrepreneurs (small shop owners, small property owners) made up only 13 percent of the total membership between 1949 and 1978, and 21 percent of those recruited in phase 1. This social group is more stable than the menu group in terms of their businesses and professions. The small entrepreneurs who joined the party during its first years constituted about 87 percent of the total entrepreneurs who joined the party between 1949 and 1978. The professionals are another important social stratum in the PSP. Approximately 60 percent of professionals joined during the first phase. Clearly, this stratum was attracted to the PSP, particularly in its early years, before Jumblatt's serious schism with the political regime. After 1958 the number of professionals joining the PSP dropped dramatically. For example, in phase 2 of the PSP development (1959-1964), only three professionals joined. It is possible that, with the hardening of the PSP's position toward the political system, the professionals realized that the party could no longer serve as a stepping-stone to public office and thus they sought other avenues to fulfill their political ambitions.[22]

Although the professionals who joined the PSP in the first phase constituted only about 1 percent of the total PSP membership for the 1949-1978 period, their political weight within the PSP far exceeded their number. They occupied virtually all PSP positions in the leadership and the delegate councils (those who assist the leadership council in running party affairs), the two highest party organs.

In phase 1, the PSP members were predominantly from rural areas (82.25 percent), and 48.19 percent of those were from Mount Lebanon, mostly from the Shouf district, Jumblatt's stronghold. Recruits from

Figure 4.2 Geographical distribution of PSP members during phase 1, 1949-1958

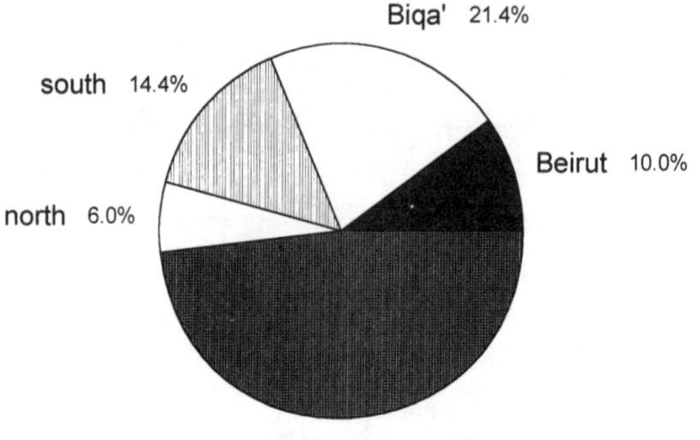

Source: PSP records

southern Lebanon made up about 14 percent, and those from the Biqa' were 21.29 percent of total recruits who joined the party during phase 1. From this geographic distribution it is clear that the party was organizing largely along the dominant/subordinate status and class axis. These areas, particularly the South and the Biqa', are predominantly Shiite, as well as the peripheral underdeveloped districts of the country. Only about 10 percent of those who joined the party in phase 1 came from the Beirut district and its urban suburbs. (See figure 4.2).

PHASE 2, 1959–1964, THE REGIME OF FOUAD SHIHAB: "CONSTRUCTIVE ENGAGEMENT"

The 1958 civil war was the first serious test of the PSP as a leftist political secular group to withstand the dynamics of sectopolitics, exacerbated by war and political factors (such as the rise in Arab nationalism, and Cold War alliances). PSP records showed that at least seventeen members were purged due to their political position during the war. Most were Christian, and some occupied high ranks in the party.[23] Other Christian members remained officially within the party but became inactive.

In contrast, the two largest groups to join the party during the period from 1959 to 1964 were the Shiite and the Druze. This was no coincidence; they also constituted the bulk of the recruits between 1959 and 1978, as the party records indicate. (See figure 4.3).

Figure 4.3 Changes in total number of new recruits, phases 1 and 2

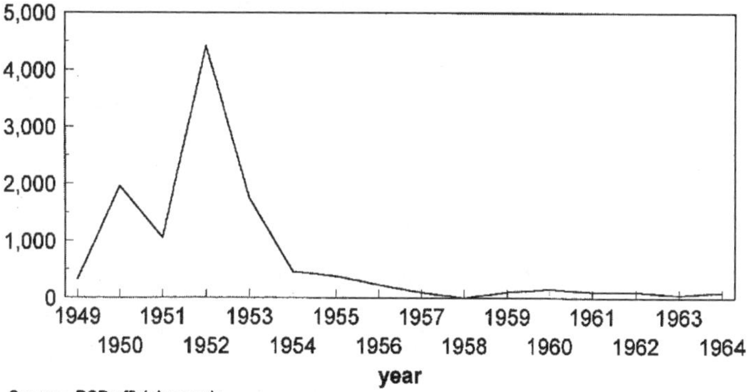

Source: PSP official records

The most logical explanation for the increase in the proportions of the Druze and Shiite is that both occupied a less privileged position than the Christians and the Sunni in Lebanon's distribution of political power. Within the subordinate Muslim group as a whole, the sects were differentiated in terms of status, with Sunni Muslims being of higher status than Druze and Shiite Muslims. It is important to mention here that the distribution of political power in Lebanon is based on the unwritten Sunni-Maronite pact, referred to as the National Pact, which gives Maronites the highest political benefits, followed by the Sunnis. The inferior status of the Shiite and the Druze pushes them to the left of the political spectrum. Hence their disproportionately high representation among the rank and file of leftist parties.[24] Christian sects also are differentiated by status. For example, Christian Orthodox, are less privileged politically than the Maronites, which explains why a large number of them also joined leftist and nationalist groups, such as the Communist Party and the Syrian Social National Party.[25]

Between 1959 and 1964 the total number of new recruits dropped to 600 members (compared to 10,500 members in phase 1). (See figure 4.4). But as discussed already, the decline in party recruitment started after 1952, following the split between Chamoun and Jumblatt. After 1958 the PSP registered a slight increase in recruits, but their number remained low when compared with the 1952 level. Several factors can explain this. The first was the inconclusive political results of the civil war, which ended in a stalemate. Disillusioned, the public became apolitical. The second reason was Jumblatt's "constructive engagement" policy with the government of Fouad Shihab. Jumblatt believed that the state could be modernized under Shihab. Shihab, a general who commanded the Lebanese army until his election in 1958, advocated a reformist agenda that relied on the modernization and strengthening of state institutions.[26] He attempted to introduce some rational-bureaucratic values to replace the sectarian clientelist political system. He thought that a rational state in the Weberian sense could better preserve the long-term interests of the Lebanese bourgeoisie. Shihab and his team were trying to address the real causes of the 1958 civil war—the political system's clientelism and sectarianism.[27]

Shihab relied on Jumblatt to realize his political program. Jumblatt was the only political boss with an important power base that had a reformist political agenda. The Shihab-Jumblatt alliance, therefore, was the result of the convergence of similar political views between two political leaders. Between 1960 and 1964, Jumblatt participated in three different cabinets cosponsored several bills for reform and development projects in the country's less-developed regions. As a result, roads were laid in about 600 villages, the Arab University was established, the Lebanese University was expanded, and the Green Plan, which included land reform and plantations, was created.[28] Furthermore, the PSP won twelve parliamentary seats in the 1960 elections. This enhanced Jumblatt's role within the political system and strengthened, at least briefly, his belief, in the constructive engagement policy.

While serving in the cabinet, Jumblatt paid little attention to the PSP, a fact that contributed to the decline in party recruitment. By the end of Shihab's presidential term, Jumblatt realized that the Lebanese state could not be modernized from within. Sectarian bosses who also represented the bourgeoisie opposed the modernization efforts, which they feared might undermine the patronage system on which their political power rested. Large segments of the Lebanese bourgeoisie (such as the Sunni Saeb Salam as well as Maronites such as Camille Chamoun, Pierre Jumayyel, and Reymond Edde) viewed the attempt to introduce legal and rational values as a loss of direct access to the clientelist structures of the Lebanese state.[29] Eventually Shihab and his successor, Charles Helou, slowed down the modernization drive, and the bosses regained their access to the state structures and institutions.

Data for this period show two major changes in the class composition of the PSP during the 1959-1964 period. (See figure 4.4). The first

Figure 4.4 Social class distribution of new members, phases 1 and 2

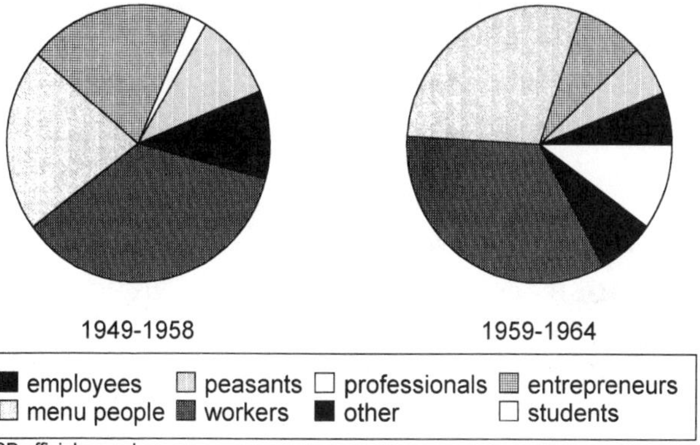

1949-1958 1959-1964

employees peasants professionals entrepreneurs
menu people workers other students

Source: PSP official records

change is the sharp decrease in the number of small entrepreneurs from 20 percent to about 8 percent. This stratum of the petty bourgeois class felt that the radical policies of the PSP did not reflect their desire for peace and political stability, which would allow them to pursue their business interests. The events of 1958 shook this stratum and henceforth determined its political behavior.

And when Jumblatt supported the Shihab's regime, the professionals were reluctant to join the PSP; only three professionals joined the party between 1959 and 1964.[30] As the PSP adopted a political line in opposition to the state, the professionals sought other avenues to fulfill their political ambitions. The constructive engagement policy, which lasted about six years, did not affect their position, as reflected by the low numbers of professionals recruited during this phase. The reluctance of the small entrepreneurs and the professionals to join the PSP could be better explained by examining their perceptions of their class interests, particularly that in the 1960s the economic boom improved the conditions of the middle class undercut radical tendencies.

In the second phase, as in the first, most of those recruited were workers and menu people. It is not surprising that the majority of members of both groups were Druze and Shiite. Their political motivation is less difficult to discern because they both belong to lower class/status groups. In this case there is an overlap between status and class, which should be analyzed more closely in connection with the political situation. In the post-1958 period, the Shiite and Druze menu people and workers probably joined the PSP for both status and class interests. They perceived the PSP as an agent of change that could alter their subordinate status both as members of certain sects, and as members of certain classes.

PHASE 3, 1965–1970: THE REGIME OF CHARLES HELOU, "THE OPPOSITION PERIOD"

Since 1965, the PSP began to change its political line based on local and regional factors. Regionally, the rise to power of the Baath Socialist Party in Syria and Iraq, the triumph of the Algerian revolution, and the political changes in Yemen, all brought about a new regional balance of forces. Jumblatt saw these regional changes in favor of the progressive social forces in Lebanon.

At the local level, labor and student unrest resurfaced again after President Shihab failed to effect social changes to correct the growing disparities among classes, sects, and regions. His regime encouraged the large-scale capitalist farming sector, which developed dramatically in light of the infrastructural improvements induced by the Litani irrigation plant and the Green Land reclamation project. This development brought new fortune to the commercial-financial bourgeoisie and misery to the peasantry. When merchants and financiers from the cities or from regional centers such as Zahle bought estates from landlords in the North, South, and the Biqa', the peasants who had worked the land were expelled. Sharecroppers, who had accounted for 25 percent of the active agrarian population in the 1950s, represented only 5 percent in 1970. Most of the rest migrated to urban areas to form the shantytowns later known as the "misery belt" that surrounded Beirut. The industrial sector absorbed only one-fifth of the rural migrants (a significant percentage of whom were Shiite); the rest joined the menu stratum.[31]

In 1965 Jumblatt called upon the Lebanese leftist parties to establish a political front. The parties that joined the Front of Progressive Parties and National Figures included the PSP, the Lebanese Communist Party, the Arab National Movement, and political figures such as parliament member Jameel Lahoud and Maarouf Saad, a populist leader from Sidon (whose assassination in 1975 triggered the civil war). The front's main task was to organize the opposition movement and to lay the foundations for a political and social reform program. But regional and local developments, such as the 1967 Arab-Israeli war and the emergence of the Palestinian resistance, overwhelmed the fragile alliance.

After the 1967 war, a new regional balance of forces crystallized; Israel emerged as the major regional power vis-à-vis Syria and Egypt. The Israeli victory affected the correlation of forces at the Lebanese level, where the antireform forces, which also opposed Arab nationalism, saw the new equation as favoring their interests.

The regional changes soon affected the PSP. In the 1968 parliamentary election it lost four seats, reducing its parliamentary caucus from twelve members to eight. Jumblatt realized the significance of a new element in Arab politics that might redress the internal Lebanese balance of forces: the Palestinian resistance. More than half a million Palestinian refugees were scattered in different refugee camps in Lebanon; this made them an important factor in the internal demographic balance between Christians and Muslims, since most of them were Muslim.

Jumblatt started furnishing an alliance with the Palestine Liberation Organization, an alliance that came to influence the Lebanese politics and conflict in the 1970s and 1980s. This alliance later became known as al "Kuwat al Mushtaraka" (the Joined Forces) of PLO and LNM during the 1975 civil war.

In terms of recruitment, regional events and the PSP policy shift from positive engagement to outright opposition helped to boost the number of new recruits. About 1,500 new members were recruited between 1965 and 1970. The PSP's increasingly active opposition in domestic affairs as well as regional changes had an impact on its sectarian composition. The distribution of new members was 695 Druze, 455 Shiite, 215 Sunni, and 106 Christians.

These figures support the claim that PSP recruitment underwent a shift during phase 2. The Druze and Shiite were the two largest groups to join the PSP. However, the Druze, who constituted about 6 percent of the total population, were overrepresented in the party. The Sunni, the third largest group to join the PSP, were attracted by Jumblatt's social activism on such issues as endorsing union demands for better salaries and improved work conditions, as well as by his support of the

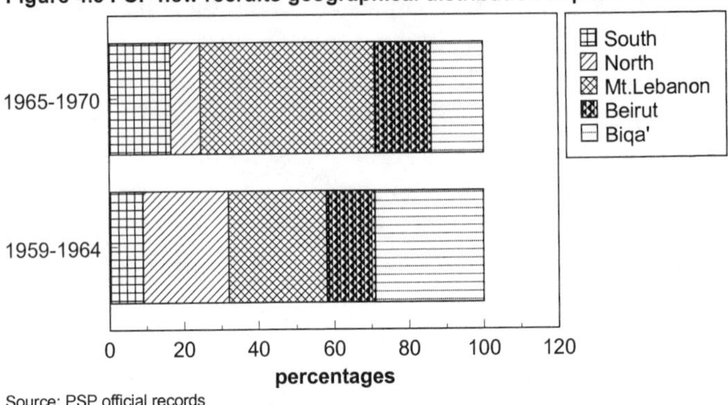

Figure 4.5 PSP new recruits geographical distribution in phases 2 and 3

Source: PSP official records

Palestinian and Arab issues. These positions enhanced his political image as a social reformer and an Arab nationalist.[32]

The PSP expanded its political recruitment in southern Lebanon. For example, in Tyre alone the PSP recruited about forty new members in phase 3, whereas it had recruited ten members from Tyre in phases 1 and 2 combined. In the entire south the PSP recruited about 250 members in phase 3, or 17 percent of the total recruited in the same period.

The members from the Biqa' district accounted for 14 percent of the total recruits during this period. Those from northern Lebanon made up about 10 percent of the total. These three districts (which are by all indices the least developed in Lebanon) together contributed about 42 percent of the total new recruits. (See figure 4.5).

This fact again supports the argument that the geographic distribution of PSP members was not coincidental but rather directly related to their background as residents of the less developed districts of Lebanon, and their sectarian makeup (Sunni, Shiite, and Druze) reflects their subordinate position.

It should be noted that in Lebanon, the three Muslim sects not only have deep theological differences, but also view each other with suspicion and subtle (and sometimes blatant) animosity. Therefore, although I discuss Muslims as a group, it does not mean that they are homogeneous. Muslims can be differentiated along status and class lines. On another level, sect members are also members of classes that are defined by their ownership (or lack of ownership) of the means of production. The attraction of the PSP for members of different sectarian backgrounds cannot be explained solely in religious terms, because that would be incompatible with their joining a multisectarian, secular, and socialist party. An approach that takes into account class and class consciousness factors provides a complementary tool to analyze the motivations of the non-Druze PSP members, the majority of those who belong to the menu stratum, working, and peasant classes.

Class interests as a motivating factor also help explain why the bourgeoisie from all sects, including the Druze, did not join the PSP between 1949 to 1978. In fact, the Druze bourgeoisie opposed the party and supported its opponent, the Arislan faction, which was closely allied with the Maronite elite and in turn was part of the antireform political establishment.

The class composition of the new recruits during the third phase included 409 menu people (27 percent), 378 students (25 percent), 307 workers (21 percent), 78 small entrepreneurs (9 percent), 33 peasants (3.8 percent), and 33 professionals (3.8 percent). This period witnessed two changes regarding the class composition of the new recruits: a decrease in the number of members belonging to the working class and an increase in the number of menu people who joined the party.

The number of recruited workers steadily declined after their record high in the first phase (3,117). Their decline is associated with the emergence of a number of leftist organizations (such as the Organization of Communist Work , the Arab Socialist Labor Party, and the Trotskites) that competed aggressively in organizing the working class. Those organizations and the Lebanese Communist Party constituted a more attractive political option to the working class than the PSP.

Students constituted 9 percent of new recruits in phase 2 and 25 percent in phase 3, a significant jump in a relatively short time. Again, their increase may be attributed to several factors. The increase in the number of public schools and the opening of the Lebanese University provided opportunities for the members of poor classes to receive free education at all levels. Muslims benefited the most from public schooling, because earlier education had been monopolized by private Christian missionary schools and universities.[33] Thus public education provided underprivileged sectors of the population with an opportunity for greater political mobilization.

More important, the PSP leadership focused on recruiting students because it recognized their political importance. Students were easier to mobilize due to their concentration in Beirut and other large cities, their higher level of political consciousness than other sectors, and their receptivity to the ideas of social and political reform. Since the mid-1960s, the PSP has targeted students in recruitment campaigns and in 1970 it created the Youth Progressive Organization, which did not require party membership. This organization, which had about 600 members in 1970, gave the party more flexibility in political mobilization and recruitment.[34]

The student movement played a leading role in the opposition in the 1960s and 1970s, and its political agenda encompassed slogans of reform and political change of the Lebanese left. The students became a focal point of political activism, manifested in strikes and demonstrations, which mirrored the general socioeconomic and political crisis then building up in the country. Therefore, it was not accidental that several Lebanese party leaders emerged from within its ranks. For example, Anwar al-Fatairy, the president of the Lebanese University student council in the late 1960s and early 1970s, rose to PSP leadership in the late 1970s. Similarly, Hisham Nasser Eddin and Tarek Shihab, both student activists, became key party leaders during the same period.[35]

On the other hand, the menu stratum continued to be substantially represented in the PSP membership, reflecting the wider process of transformation occurring in the social production process, where an increasing number of peasants were added to this stratum. Lebanon's service economy has increasingly transformed the country's economic structure; by the 1970s this sector contributed about 70 percent of the gross national product, which meant that most of the nation's workforce was tied up with the service economy.[36] Thus it is no coincidence that the PSP and many other Lebanese parties relied on the support of this significant social group.

Members of the menu people have distinct class characteristics, including their strong ties with their rural background and family, customs, norms, and belief systems, which in turn shape their political culture and ideological orientation. The menu people are largely individualistic in their behavior and work ethics, a trait derived from their peasant lifestyle; living in isolated self-contained social entities, they had little contact with other peasants or with the world beyond their own village.[37] These characteristics help explain the group's sectopolitical consciousness; sectopolitics affected the way in which they identified themselves and others as well as the political choices they made. This is of particular interest since the menu people constitute the majority of PSP members recruited since 1965. It came to constitute the backbone of the different militias that developed after 1975.

PHASE 4: PRELUDE TO THE CIVIL WAR, 1971–1975

In 1970 the Lebanese parliament elected Sleiman Franjieh president of the republic. His election brought an official end to Shihabism and to the reform attempts from within the political system. Franjieh, a large landowner from Zgharta in northern Lebanon, represented the anti-reform segment of the Lebanese ruling class.[38] He sought to reinforce the power of the traditional political bosses that Shihab, and, to a lesser extent, his successor President Charles Helou, tried to curtail.[39] Franjieh's election indicated how resistant the political bosses to change; put another way, by electing Franjieh, the sectarian bosses reinforced their position within the political system. Paradoxically, the PSP representatives in parliament cast their votes for Franjieh, who won by one vote over his competitor, Elyas Sarkis, a Shihabist. While contradicting the party's political platform, the PSP position demonstrates the extent of PSP disenchantment with Shihabism, which failed to bring about meaningful political change. In other words, the PSP vote should not be seen as a sign of support of Franjieh but rather as a rejection of the Shihab experiment.

The PSP's policy of opposition during the Franjieh regime supports this argument. Since the mid-1960s, the PSP played an active role in forging an alliance between all opposition forces in the country, which resulted in the Front of Progressive Parties and national figures. The front was a loose alliance without a defined structural organization, but this was soon remedied by the creation of the Lebanese National Movement (LNM), which for the first time institutionalized the alliance.

The LNM created its own organizational structures such as the central committee (al-Majlis al-Siyasi-al-Markazi), which was chaired by

Jumblatt; a daily newspaper; and a security force. Such institutions helped the leftist parties attain a higher level of political coordination and organization. Jumblatt played a pivotal role in laying the foundations for this alliance of Arab Nationalists, Communists, Baathists, and liberal independents. His intellectual depth and charismatic personality overcame the political and ideological differences among them.[40]

The PSP's leading role in the opposition and Jumblatt's growing stature did not really affect the party's sectarian composition. Although that the secular and democratic reform program articulated by Jumblatt and adopted by the alliance might have been expected to attract a wider Christian audience, this did not occur. On the contrary, the number of Christians recruited between 1971 and 1975 decreased from the previous phase: Only seventy-six Christians joined the party, and most were Orthodox Armenians belonging to the menu stratum. The number of Christians accounted for about 6 percent of the total recruits during this phase.[41]

Clearly then, the PSP, like other Lebanese leftist groups, could not overcome the structural limitations imposed by the sectarian system of domination and its far-reaching political effects on Lebanon's sects. The system of domination coupled with sectopolitics separated the different religious communities and largely determined their political allegiance. The position of sects in the hierarchy of power becomes a key to understand the sects' political behavior.

In their recruitment efforts, the Kataib Party and other rightist groups relied principally on sectarian slogans and propaganda to attract the Christian population, particularly the Maronites. The Amal Movement, which emerged in the mid-1970s, followed similar methods to recruit and mobilize Shiites. The sectopolitical campaigns of the Kataib and the Amal movement prevented the PSP from expanding its power base within these two communities.

The number of new Shiite members started to stagnate in the 1970s, when the Amal movement emerged. Thus, it may be concluded that the emergence of Amal, a strictly Shiite organization, has made it more difficult for the PSP to attract Shiite members. The emergence of Amal also came at a time when sectopolitics assumed greater importance (particularly after the mid-1970s). Since 1975 Lebanon has been divided largely along sectopolitical lines.

The numbers of Sunnis in the PSP increased by about 5 percent from the previous phase. They amounted to about 20 percent of those recruited in phase 4. A significant number of them were inhabitants of the Maslakh and Carantina shantytowns; many were Arab gypsies who were not Lebanese citizens. Jumblatt supported their demand for citizenship and in return received their political support. The majority of Sunnis were from the urban menu stratum.

The recruited Druze amounted to about 50 percent of the total during this phase, representing an increase of 3 percent from the previous phase. This was the highest percentage attained of Druze members since the party's inception. In real figures the number of Druze declined from 695 recruited members in phase 3 to 687 in phase 4. Thus, although the number of Druze did not actually increase, they formed a larger percentage of the total because the number of Christians and Shiite recruits decreased.

The class composition of PSP members recruited in phase 4 revealed a pattern begun in phase 3. The students, the single largest group, amounted to about 32 percent of those recruited. The second group was that of the menu people, which amounted to 24 percent of all members. The students and the menu people composed about 56 percent of those recruited in this phase. This marked a shift in the class distribution of recruited members away from the working class, which composed 35 percent and 34 percent of all members recruited during each of the preceding phases. The political implications of this shift in the social class composition of the recruited members is important, particularly if taken in connection with other sociopolitical developments. The PSP adopted a policy to widen its support base within the student movement, which in the mid-1960s became more politicized and influenced by leftist ideologies.

Jumblatt paid attention to the student movement; his party used the university forum effectively to attract party members. Several PSP leaders indicated that their first exposure to PSP political views came at a panel discussion or lecture at their school.[42] Jumblatt's intellectualism and his special brand of socialism appealed to students who were less attracted to Marxism-Leninism. Most of the party leaders and cadres interviewed refused to join the Communist Party due to its atheist ideology, whereas the PSP brand of socialism emphasized the value of religion, making it more relevant to their own value system.[43] This fact in turn sheds light on the ideological values of those students who joined the PSP, the children of a society in which religion occupies a central place in the value system.

Why did the menu people join the party at an increasing rate in proportion to other classes and strata? The first explanation for this is the economic insecurities of this stratum, which increased in the 1960s due to the growing economic crisis. The menu people perceived the PSP as their passport for jobs. In this connection it should be remembered that Jumblatt was not only the leader of a political party but also a leader and representative of the Druze within the Lebanese sectarian system. This entitled him to appoint a certain number of employees within the government bureaucracy. The menu stratum wanted Jumblatt to use his leverage to find them any job—or even cash—available.

On Saturdays and Sundays, Jumblatt received hundreds of people soliciting jobs, most of them from the menu stratum. To them he usually gave a card carrying his personal signature, to be given to the person in charge at the institution or bureaucracy where a job was available. In return for this favor many jobhunters became PSP members.

As mentioned earlier, the political behavior of the menu stratum is largely individualistic due to their transitional nature, composed of uprooted peasants who had not been economically relocated. It is a floating social group that can be found in many Third World societies.

In this phase, workers constituted about 23 percent of those recruited. Although their numbers declined, they are still important because of their relatively high percentage among all recruits. Most of the workers were the first-generation offspring of peasants; many retained ownership of small pieces of property. Therefore, these workers cannot be considered proletarized (dispossessed of all types of ownership). The workers recruited by the PSP were predominantly from rural areas and commuted to their jobs in the cities. Most of the Lebanese working class worked in family-owned workshops that employed five or less workers.[44] This fact made it unlikely that they would develop class consciousness, because the owners usually are involved in the production process in family workshops and so workers may not sense class differences between themselves and the owners.

Moreover, limited contact with other workers inhibits the development of class solidarity. In summary, then, the three most important social groups—the menu stratum, students, and workers—that joined the PSP share important characteristics, such as rural peasant backgrounds and small landholdings; this background helps explain the extent of their class consciousness prior to their recruitment by the PSP.

The stratum of small entrepreneurs constituted about 5 percent of those recruited in phase 4, a rate that had declined since phase 1, at which time they constituted 21 percent of recruits. The reasons for this decline were discussed in phase 2 and are valid for phases 3 and 4 as well. The class interests of this group determined to a large extent its political stance toward the PSP. The small entrepreneurs were suspicious of the PSP's socialist orientation. They were more inclined to support the free enterprise economic system in hopes that they might improve their chances for upward class mobility rather than support social change that might jeopardize their interests.

The professionals, too, shared the same suspicions. In 1975-1976, only twenty-five professionals joined the party, most of whom were engineers educated at the expense of the PSP in Eastern Bloc countries.[45] Those professionals were mostly children of menu people families—that is, of different class backgrounds from the professionals who had joined the PSP in its first two phases.

Another important social group that became increasingly represented among the ranks of the new recruits was the private and public sector employee. These two groups were predominantly clerks, hotel and restaurant employees, security guards, bank tellers, and the like, the so-called modern segment of the petty bourgeois class.[46] In the first phase, employees constituted about 5 percent of those recruited, whereas in phase 2 they constituted about 9 percent; in phase 3 16 percent; and in phase 4, they constituted about 13 percent. The employees, mostly of peasant backgrounds, had succeeded in acquiring primary and secondary education, which allowed them to find jobs in the service sector or to work in the government bureaucracy. A number of those acquired their positions via the *wasta* system, that is, through the favors provided by the political bosses, such as Jumblatt, to their clientele. Thus those employees are part of the constituency built by Jumblatt and his party. Therefore, their recruitment should be seen within the context of clientelism, which is intricately related with the Lebanese sectarian system of quotas. A parallel system also runs in the private sector, where businessmen respect the general rules of sectarian quotas without necessarily considering them binding, as they are in the public sector.

In the private sector the game becomes more complex when *wasta* comes into play. The *wasta* system benefits businessmen and the boss. The first always keeps in mind that gaining the support of the boss is more useful than provoking his anger. After all, businessmen might need the support for a bill in parliament, to win the government's approval for an import/export license, to acquire a government concession. While Jumblatt was the least involved in the *wasta* system due to his politics, government in power and the private sector always tried to contain his revolution by employing his political supporters.

In summary, the social classes and strata that joined the PSP during phase 4 were of peasant origins. These social groups generally were influenced by power arrangements, sectopolitics, and changing economic conditions.

PHASE 5: THE CIVIL WAR AND ITS AFTERMATH, 1976–1977

The civil war, which began on April 13, 1975, was the outcome of the conjunction of domestic socioeconomic and political crises with international and regional factors that had been building up since the early 1960s. The war brought to the surface the limitations of the political system. More than ever before, the Lebanese sectarian political system and its socioeconomic structures were unable to accommodate the social and political needs of most Lebanese.

The system of domination and the hierarchical sectarian structure unwittingly created the elements of its own destruction by polarizing people along sectarian lines, thanks to sectopolitics. The system failed to gain the consent of the civil society, particularly its deprived Muslim component. The Muslim elite revolted in order to introduce structural changes in the distribution of political power encouraged by the PLO's armed presence in Lebanon.

At another level, the civil war drastically changed the structures and functions of political parties in Lebanon. The most important change was the parties' militarization; their organizational setup required adjustments and changes to accommodate the needs of war.

The Lebanese civil war was fought largely along conventional lines where the combatants used all types of weaponry and engaged in conventional war strategies.

Most Lebanese parties, particularly those of the left, were ill-prepared to fight this type of war. They were more prepared to a guerrilla type of war. That is why in the early months of the fighting, the Palestinian resistance, which was better trained and equipped for this kind of warfare, played a major role. This subject is beyond the scope of the present study, but what is relevant here is that the scope and the intensity of the war required that the PSP and other parties introduce militia into their organizational composition.

The PSP militia recruited people at a mass level, undermining the traditional party procedures of organizing membership. Militia members were not required to join the party and were not subject to the party's political education process.[47] Militia leaders were party members but were mostly among the working members; very few were advising members. This allowed the rank-and-file members to assume military responsibilities which far exceeded those assumed by members of the upper party echelons.

The PSP succeeded in creating a militia with several thousand members in a relatively short time. This helped military leaders to become important actors within the party, even if their official party rank was only that of a member or working member. In fact, the party's ranking system, which organized its recruits hierarchically as members, working members, and advising members. began to become obsolete.[48] While this created chaos within party ranks, Kamal Jumblatt kept it within tolerable limits.[49]

Party militarization occurred gradually. At first, military personnel assumed the responsibility for local party branches and the Moutamadiyat. (A *moutamadiya* is composed of two or more branches). Prior to 1975, branch directors were civilians with no military expertise and were subject to continuous political education; each branch had regular meetings every fifteen days. During those meetings a high-ranking party official lectured about the party's doctrine and other political issues. Moreover, branch members were required to attend the cadre school if they wished to be raised from member to working member, or from working member to advising member. The cadre school was design to teach the party's socialist doctrine and political line.[50]

From 1975 to 1977 the party cadre school was suspended, which compromised the political education of party members, including new recruits.[51] Thus the new recruits were not subject to the same ideological and political education as those recruited prior to the civil war. This fact is important, particularly when noting the social and sectarian backgrounds of those who joined the party after 1975. Most belonged to the menu stratum or were students.

Jumblatt himself was the top commander and supervised the PSP's overall military strategy and strategic goals. But this did not prevent the military from building its own power base in its areas of operations. Militia members developed allegiance to their military leaders, who provided favors, such as extra family allowances and benefits. Gradually, the militia lieutenants became "bosses," with a *wasta* system and clientelism that paralleled that of the Lebanese political system and the social relations it created.

The PSP military cadres were predominantly rural, young, and Druze. Their class and sectarian makeup contributed to the ongoing transformation of the PSP's social composition. Gradually party membership came to draw heavily on the Muslim (and especially Druze) menu stratum. The military also transformed the party by eroding the civilian political organizational structures that had existed prior to 1975. The party's increasing militarization contributed to its continuous low recruitment rates among the Christian community.

In phase 5, Christians constituted 5 percent of total recruits, maintaining the same percentage as during phase 4. This fact indicates that in time of crisis, the Christians were recruited in low numbers, such as in the (pre–civil war) 1953-1958 phase. They also were not recruited successfully in the years prior to the 1975 civil war, when social and political tensions were rising. The few Christians who entered the PSP in 1976 and 1977 did so to avoid persecution, particularly since most of them lived in areas under the control of the PSP forces.

Sunni members amounted to 22 percent of those recruited in this phase. Most were from the Eqleem al-Kharoub in the Shouf Mountains. The Eqleem is part of the Shouf electorate district. In 1970 the party launched a recruitment campaign there in an effort to help the parliamentary election of Zaher al-Khatib, son of Anwar al-Khatib (a member of leadership council and a parliament member). As a result of this campaign, several Sunni from the Eqleem joined the PSP. Similarly

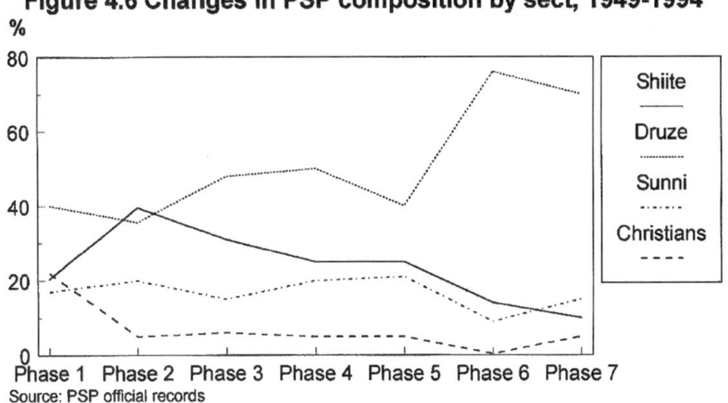

Figure 4.6 Changes in PSP composition by sect, 1949-1994

to the previous phase, the Shiite constituted 25 percent of those recruited and the Druze, 49 percent.

During this phase, the Druze, Shiite, and Sunni members continued to form a majority, thus reinforcing the sectarian composition trend that began in phase 2. (See figure 4.6). This trend reveals that the subordinate group, the Muslims, were more attracted to the PSP as a reformist, secular political party. And it also shows that the Christians were joining the party in decreasing numbers particularly after the 1953 Chamoun-Jumblatt split. To a large degree, the sectopolitical factor influenced those trends. In times of crisis (1958 and 1975), when sectopolitical agitation was at its peak, fewer Christians joined the PSP than was during times of relative political stability (such as during the years from 1949 to 1952). The Muslims reacted differently to crisis: They maintained rather stable percentages. For example, the Druze constituted 48 percent, 50 percent, and 49 percent of those recruited in phases 3, 4, and 5 respectively, while the Shiite constituted 31 percent, 25 percent, and 24 percent. As explained before, the decline in the Shiite proportions was due to the emergence of the Amal Shiite movement. Thus, the decline in the proportion of Shiites joining the PSP in phases 4 and 5 could be attributed to sectopolitics. The Sunni recruits, on the other hand, constituted 15 percent, 20 percent, and 21 percent of those recruited in phases 3, 4, and 5. The steady increase in the Sunni membership is not related to sectarian polarization, but the data on the Sunni members' areas of origins suggest other factors were behind this

TABLE 4.3.
CHANGES IN CONFESSIONAL COMPOSITION OF PSP MEMBERSHIP DURING PHASES 1 TO 5: PERCENTAGE OF CHRISTIAN, DRUZE, SHIITE AND SUNNI MEMBERS OF ALL RECRUITS.

PHASE	CHRISTIAN	DRUZE	SHIITE	SUNNI	TOTAL
1	22.0	40.4	20.3	17.3	100%
2	4.7	35.6	39.6	20.1	100%
3	7.2	47.3	30.9	14.6	100%
4	5.5	50.0	24.8	19.7	100%
5	5.3	47.5	24.5	21.7	100%

Source: PSP official records.

trend: In phase 3, Jumblatt's support of the predominantly Sunni shanty dwellers of Maslakh and Carantina increased the PSP popularity among them; and in phases 4 and 5, the PSP paid attention to the Eqleem al-Kharoub, an area predominantly inhabited by Sunni. (See table 4.3).

The Druze, particularly those of menu stratum background, were increasingly attracted to the PSP for two main reasons. First, the party, particularly in times of economic crisis, was perceived as a provider of jobs and favors for its members and supporters. Second, when sectopolitical propaganda increased, the Druze reacted by joining "Jumblatt's party"; they viewed the PSP as the defender of their faith. During the 1958 and 1975 crises, Druze support of Jumblatt increased. But not all Druze reacted similarly; members of the menu stratum and the students, for instance, joined the party in largest numbers. This was true of the Sunni and Shiite communities also. This fact confirms the intertwined relationship between class and status. The upper segments of the petty bourgeoisie (such as the entrepreneurs and professionals) as well as the bourgeoisie classes of all sects, including the Druze, did not join or support the PSP.

PHASE 6 (1978–1979): THE PARTY AFTER THE DEATH OF ITS FOUNDER

On March 16, 1977, Kamal Jumblatt was assassinated near his hometown of al-Moukhtara in the Shouf Mountains. His death tested the party's ability to survive without the guidance of its founder and leader of more than twenty-eight years. The PSP went through an uneasy leadership transition process. Although most officials interviewed did not feel comfortable talking about the intricacies of the transition, all focused on the challenge of choosing a new leader without losing the PSP's main base of support, the Druze. The vice president of the PSP, Fareed Jubran (a Christian), said in an interview that since the Druze constituted an important support base, the most logical successor was Walid, Kamal Jumblatt's only son. Jubran explained that some party leaders objected to his nomination, but eventually a majority reached an agreement and Walid became the new leader.[52]

Jubran's argument was well grounded; in less than a year a record 1,122 Druze entered the party, constituting about 76 percent of those recruited in 1978. The party's Druze base increased after the death of Jumblatt, an expected reaction to the loss of the group's most prominent and distinguished leader. The number of recruited Sunni members decreased from 22 percent of the total in phase 5 to 9 percent of all recruits in phase 6. The Shiite members amounted to about 14 percent of those recruited in phase 6, a decrease from 24 percent in the previous phase. Only six new Christian members joined the PSP in 1978, comprising about 0.41 percent of all those recruited in that same year.

Therefore, after Kamal Jumblatt's assassination, the PSP became a party with a clear Druze majority. Many factors contributed to this shift in the party's sectarian composition; certainly the 1975-1976 civil war shows concretely the use of sectopolitics as a mean to mobilize sects. The Lebanese left, although an opposing ideological force to sectopolitics, mobilized few Christians but managed to recruit larger numbers of Muslims, whose political and social status was lower than of the Christians. The Lebanese right, which sought to maintain the political status quo, mobilized the predominant status group, the Christian Maronites.

The sectopolitical polarization of the Lebanese masses, particularly after the civil war and the accompanying sectarian massacres overshadowed class consciousness. The Druze believed that their self-defense depended on their allegiance to Jumblatt's party. This partly explains why more Druze joined after 1977 than at any time. Other sects mirrored the Druze political behavior. Both the Shiite and Sunni joined political movements of a sectarian nature, such as the Amal Shiite movement and the Mourabiton Sunni movement. Of course, the Maronites under the leadership of the Kataib Party were subject to sectarian mobilization long before the Muslims.

The class distribution of those who joined the PSP in 1978 included a majority of high school students (31 percent) and the menu stratum (28 percent). In other words, these two groups were the most sensitive to sectopolitics. Students' party membership increased remarkably during the 1970s, which coincided with the mounting social tensions and the corresponding sectopolitical polarization. The students who joined the PSP since 1970 amounted to about 62 percent of all students who joined the party for the entire 1949 to 1978 phase.

Although menu stratum membership declined since phase 2, it never constituted less than 20 percent of total recruits in any phase; this group's party membership began to increase after 1976 and throughout the civil war, until it constituted 29 percent of the total, as it had during phase 2.

The number of workers joining the PSP started to decline after phase 3, at which time they amounted to 21 percent of all recruits; in phase 5 they were only 15 percent and in phase 6, 13 percent. Clearly, an inverse relationship exists between the increase in sectopolitical polarization and the workers' membership in the PSP. The number of recruited workers decreased from its preceding level at two important junctures. For instance, phase 5, the number of recruited workers declined from 22 percent in phase 4 to 15 percent in phase 5. This came at a time when sectopolitical consciousness was at its peak. In phase 6, when sectopolitical polarization also played a definite role in the recruitment process, the percentage of workers decreased to 13 percent of all recruits, the lowest it ever fell since the party's inception in 1949. This observation is further supported by the high number of workers (3,717) who joined the party during phase 1. They constituted 75 percent of all workers joining the PSP between 1949 and 1978. Furthermore, during the first three years of phase 1 (1949-1952), sectopolitical polarization was at its ebb in Lebanon. It is interesting to note that the working-class membership was also low in other Lebanese parties, such as the Kataib Party, which mobilized members along sectarian lines.[53]

The data collected from the PSP official records covering 1949 to 1994 present three main patterns in members' class and sectarian distribution. The first pattern is that in times of heightened sectopolitical polarization, Muslims joined the party in higher proportions than Christians. Second, sectopolitical polarization also affected Muslim sects; the proportions of Shiites who joined the party decreased after the establishment of the Amal Shiite movement, which targeted them exclusively. Third, there exists a significant difference in the membership pattern of the different classes. At every juncture of high sectarian polarization, the number of workers decreased while numbers of students and menu people membership increased. Examples of these patterns are given below.

In phase 3 (1965-1970), for example, the proportion of Druze recruits was about 12 percent higher than it had been in phase 2. This increase is attributed to several factors, first among them being the increased polarization in the country after Jumblatt shifted gears from "constructive engagement" to outright opposition of the political regime. The second part of the 1960s was largely characterized by sectarian polarization. In 1968 a tripartite coalition among the most prominent Maronite leaders, Reymond Edde, Camille Chamoun, and Pierre Jumayyel, attested to this polarization. The shifts in the realignment of forces in Lebanon and the winds of change blowing from the region, particularly after the Israeli-Arab war of 1967, led Jumblatt to pay extra attention to his party after a phase of neglect. These two factors resulted in the mobilization of his Druze power base.

Moreover, the data reveal that Druze were recruited in the largest proportions in 1978, immediately after Kamal Jumblatt's assassination. Certainly sectarian mobilization played an important role in phase 6. Sectopolitics played a significant role in shaping the sectarian distribution of PSP membership in other phases as well. Statistical analysis of the data indicates a significant difference in the distribution of new recruits by sect between 1949 and 1978 (chi square = 1482.4, DF = 15, and p <0.0000). However, this sectarian distribution of members varied in intensity and in the nature of its sectarian characteristics. (See figure 4.6).

At the class distribution level, the number of workers decreased at every point of heightened sectarian polarization. On the other hand, the percentages of students and menu people increased, particularly in times of sectopolitical polarization. There was a statistically significant difference in the distribution of new recruits by class (chi square = 4769.114, DF = 55, p <0.000). (See figure 4.7).

Figure 4.7 PSP membership by social class phases 1 to 6

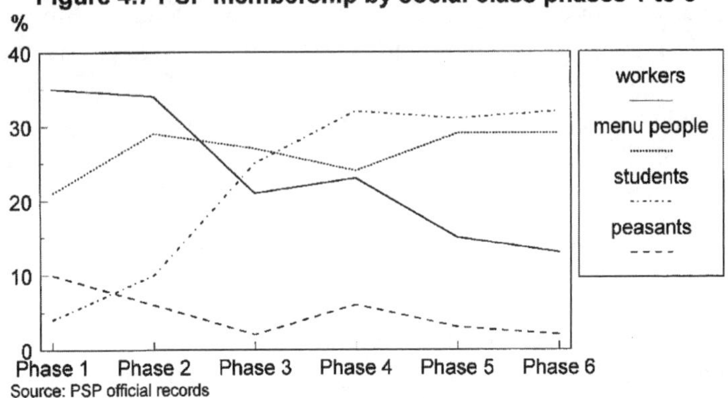

Source: PSP official records

Therefore, as data analysis indicates, the class and sectarian distribution of recruited PSP members between the 1949 and 1978 was not by chance. Members' class and sectarian distribution are variables that are directly influenced by the structure of power and mediated by socioeconomic and ideological (sectopolitics) variables.

The trends noted above were reinforced during the 1980-1994 period (phase 7), as the party continued its gravitation toward sectopolitics. The Druze support base of the party was widened while the party failed to attract members of other sects. By 1994 70 percent of the PSP members were Druze. The remaining members were distributed as follows: 15 percent were Sunni; 10 percent were Shiite; and 5 percent, Christians. About 80 percent of those members are from lower class origins, particularly from the menu people.[54] There is no sign that the PSP will be able to recover any time soon the secular credentials it once claimed, particularly in its multisectarian support base. In 1998 it was reported that PSP membership amounted to 26,000.[55]

CHAPTER FIVE

The PSP during the Years of Turmoil and Reconciliation, 1979–1996

IN EXPLAINING THE FACTORS that allowed these recruitment trends to take hold of the PSP, it is imperative to illuminate the political choices the PSP made between 1979 and 1996. After assuming the party's leadership, Walid Jumblatt made rallying the Druze support his top priority. This political choice undermined the party's standing as a secular force in the body politics of Lebanon. The prime victim of that policy was the PSP alliance with the other leftist parties of the Lebanese National Movement (LNM), which was strained and finally faltered in 1983.

The collapse of the LNM, the umbrella of the leftist alliance, weakened the standing of all secular forces and contributed to making sectopolitics the dominant political discourse in Lebanon. The PSP stood to lose most of its prestige and influence, which the party had cultivated during its three-decade-long leadership of the Lebanese left. In the 1980s, the PSP emerged more than ever before as a sectarian political force (i.e., in terms of its base of support and political actions), joining the ranks of the Kataib, the Lebanese Forces, Amal movement, and the Party of God (a Shiite organization established in 1983).

The political choices of the PSP leadership (particularly Jumblatt's decision to consolidate his Druze base) in the post-1978 phase contributed to the acceleration of the sectarian conflict in the country. In hindsight, the party overlooked its commitment to secularism just when it was needed the most. After all, choices of elites do matter, even if those choices are constrained by structural, institutional, and other political conditions.

Two observations are in order to explain some motives behind Walid Jumblatt's political behavior. One is that he was a novice political leader and lacked the intellectual depth and experience of his father, and he was less committed to secularism.[1] This can explain his drive to secure his Druze base first, rather than focusing on expanding the party's popular base. The second factor was his father's assassination, which affected his political course particularly in avoiding any confrontation with Syrian plans in Lebanon and by keeping a low profile in national politics. It is widely believed that the Syrian regime was behind the assassination of his father, who opposed Syria's invasion of Lebanon.[2] Unwittingly, Jumblatt's political choices and concerns in the first years of his leadership had severe repercussions in the years that followed.[3]

In 1982 Israel invaded Lebanon, introducing a new, volatile element into the ongoing Lebanese crisis. Segments of the Maronite elite, which had an alliance with Israel,[4] thought that this was their chance to reinforce their political hegemony over Lebanon.[5] Accordingly, when the Israeli armed forces invaded, the Maronite elite provided needed political cover and assistance.

The Israeli army placed the Lebanese Forces, the militia of the Kataib and other rightist groups, in the heartland of the Druze regions in Mount Lebanon. The Israelis' intention was to play both groups against each other in order to exercise political leverage on the two. Israel desired the Druze support for its policy in Lebanon, particularly for a peace treaty that would secure Israel strategic interests in Lebanon and in the region, given that the Druze community is also an important social group in Syria. Israel had already secured the endorsement of a good segment of the Maronite elite to its plan, thus gaining over the Druze was essential to tip the balance for its favor. The PSP resisted the Israel plan, which put the Druze on a collision course with the Maronite rightist militias.

From its alliance with Israel, the Maronite elite hoped to secure political hegemony in Lebanon. This resonated with President Chamoun's 1958 attempt to achieve the same objective by establishing an alliance with Western countries.[6] Henceforth, the stage was set for a new round of sectarian conflict after the belligerent forces decided again to settle their power struggle by violent means.

As mentioned before, prior to 1982 Jumblatt concentrated on his Druze base; finally his policy paid off. By 1982 he succeeded in positioning himself as the main figure within his sect, overshadowing his contenders in the Arislan Druze faction. When the Israeli forces placed Lebanese Forces in the Druze areas, the PSP was already equipped organizationally to launch an all-out war against them. Interestingly, Israel did not disarm the PSP, which facilitated the party's mobilization of the Druze.

In September 1983 Israel repositioned its forces and withdrew from Mount Lebanon. This signaled the beginning of the so-called Mountain War between the Druze and the Maronite Lebanese Forces. The result was a bloodbath and another chapter to be added to the sectarian conflict. The ferocity of the war and the massacres committed by both sides diminished the secular option in Lebanon. The Mountain War marked a turning point for two main reasons: First, it completed the process of "sectarian cleansing" by ending the intersectarian mixing in villages and cities that were affected by the conflict prior to 1982. The second point is the political ramification of creating "pure areas" on intersectarian relations in general and the future of building political organization that cross-cuts sectarian divides. Undoubtedly both factors placed additional obstacles in front of any future secular political organization and the building of democracy.

In the aftermath of the Mountain War, the sectarian strife took sharp turns and political chaos reigned over Lebanon after the so-called 6 of February Revolt, which subjected west Beirut to the militia rules of the PSP and the Amal Movement; the eastern suburbs were under the control of the Lebanese Forces. The 1983 to 1989 phase was perhaps the most complex and violent in the conflict's history, due to the acceleration of regional and international intervention and the political dynamics of the conflict itself.

New political actors emerged, such as the Shiite Party of God, a client of Iran; the Iraqi-supported General Michel Oun, who assumed the position of prime minister (1988-1990) at the end of Amin Jumayyel's presidency. These two actors played a significant political role particularly in changing the battle lines from Muslim/Christian to intrasectarian conflict, in which actors competed for supremacy within their own sects. The Party of God battled the Amal Movement relentlessly for the supremacy within the Shiite community. The Lebanese Forces, in turn, were consumed by internal conflicts and factional warfare, which culminated into a full-scale war with the forces of General Oun in 1988-1989. The exploration of these conflicts and their effect on the power structures within the sects is pivotal but not within the scope of this study; suffice it to say that these intrasectarian wars ushered in a new phase in the Lebanese conflict that brought new faces into the ruling political elite. Chapter 6 elaborates on the causes and the implications of intrasectarian war on the party politics in Lebanon.

These conflicts were the culmination of a long process unleashed by the 1975 civil war that set the stage for political change. The militia leaders and the war system[7] that they instituted provided them with the resources (financial, military, and the constituency) to alter the balance of power within their own sects. This allowed the emergence of political leaders such as Samir Jaja, the leader of the Lebanese Forces; Elie Hubeika, a former leader of the LF and currently a member of the parliament and cabinet; George Saadeh, the leader of the Kataib Party; Nabih Berri, the leader of Amal Movement and the house speaker (1990-). Those new leaders are from rural origins and from lower-middle-class backgrounds and, except for Saadeh, who ascended to the leadership due to inner party mechanisms, owe their ascendance to power to the war, because participation in militias facilitated their upward political mobility. Before the 1975 civil war, the exclusionary and highly elitist nature of Lebanon's political system frustrated the aspirations of the lower and middle classes for a wider political participation.

The Druze community at large did not undergo a significant change in power structure; at least at the surface, it appears that the Jumblatt and the Arislan clans are in control of the political process. This is in sharp contrast with the violent processes that the Shiite, Maronite, and to a lesser extent the Sunni community had to go through during the uneasy birth of a new leadership. Perhaps the most plausible explanation why the Druze did not witness a change in their traditional leadership can be attributed to PSP success in channeling and expressing the interests of the middle- and lower-middle-class Druze. The wide support that the party enjoys in these two sectors validates this observation.

A second plausible explanation is that the bipolar leadership system of the Druze provided an element of stability for the power structure that extended for a few centuries. The Arislan/Jumblatt factions inherited power from the Druze Kaisi/Yemeni factions of the sixteenth century. Over the years the two factions have held virtual hegemony over the community, including the appointment of its clergy. (See chapter 3).

The third contributing factor is the Druze psyche and political culture, which are typical of minorities who fear that the least provocation threatens their very existence. This feeling is underpinned by suspicion of the intentions of other communities, which stems from Druze history as a heterodox Muslim community that has been persecuted since the twelfth century, when their sect emerged in the midst of an opposing Sunni majority.

In this context, the Druze perceive political change as destabilizing because it can weaken the community's abilities to defend itself vis-à-vis the "perceived threat," particularly if that change is one of leadership, which can trigger intrasect conflicts. These feelings and perceptions were reinforced after the death of Kamal Jumblatt and the events that ensued, including among other things, the Mountain War, which raised the specter of danger to the very existence of the Druze community.

Finally, the political system based on sectarian representation has reinforced the traditional power structures by maintaining them as the main channel by which the Druze are politically represented. The traditional social structures, in turn, consolidate and legitimize the sectarian political system.

Notwithstanding the relative stability of the Druze power structure, there are some signs of strains and indicators of change. In the 1992 and 1996 elections, some Druze candidates ran for the election as independents, challenging both the traditional norms and the candidates supported by the Druze chieftains. Druze political aspirants are increasingly seeking new avenues for political mobility rather than the traditional ones of Jumblatt and Arislan.[8] At another level, there is an increasing growth of local organizations and neighborhood groups in Druze villages and cities, which transcend and at times even challenge the traditional lines of authority and circuits of family patriarchs and local notables (followers of either faction) in their activities.[9] This development could suggest that a slow erosion of authority is taking place. The overall processes of change taking place within other sects can accelerate this erosion.

Paradoxically, the PSP has inadvertently contributed to the power erosion of the traditional leadership, which occurred by providing a political space for leaders coming from lower- and middle-class origins.

In the 1992 and 1996 elections, at least two (out of four) members of the PSP parliamentary bloc were of lower-class origins. Such a development cracked the edifice of traditional power circles formed by the network of prominent Druze families, generating social tensions between traditional families and the emerging ones.

In some major cities, such as Aley, Baysour, and Sheweifat (the largest city in the district of Aley), some PSP members aspired to run for mayor, a position that was reserved for decades for prominent notables. Traditional political families as well as some independent Druze civic leaders detest this development. Nonetheless, if the current trends continue, the hegemony of the Jumblatt and Arislan factions will gradually collapse.

In the 1996 parliamentary elections, the PSP (four seats) and its allies (eight seats) won twelve seats, allowing it to become one of the largest parliamentary blocs. Jumblatt's success is attributed to two main factors: one was Syrian support, and the second was his ability to use the PSP organizational base and his traditional Druze base to establish its dominant position. The 1996 election demonstrated the weakness of the Arislan Druze faction; if not for Syrian pressures and Jumblatt's acquiescence, the only parliamentary seat it won in the Aley district by its neophyte leader, Talal Arislan, could not have been possible.

Paradoxically, however, in 1960 the PSP succeeded also in winning 12 seats and formed the largest bloc. The difference is that in 1960, the party ran at the national level in four *muhafazat* out of five, while in the 1996 elections, its bloc came from Mount Lebanon. This fact illustrates two things—first, the PSP role has increased as a sectopolitical force with successful alliances with traditional Christian political families from Aley and the Shouf. Second, the PSP gains were obtained within the parameters drawn by the sectopolitical arrangement of Taif and not as a force of social and political change, as was the case in the 1960s.

SECTOPOLITICS UNDER TAIF

The emergence of new leaders or the persistence of some traditional ones did not alter the fundamental nature of the conflict between the Muslim and Maronite elites. In fact, intrasectarian conflicts (Amal Movement–Party of God, LF-LF, and LF–General Oun) were underpinned by their claims that they were the "guardians" of their respective sect's interests. Although these intrasectarian wars exhausted the belligerent forces, no significant change was evident in terms of these leaders' positions toward the then existing power arrangement. The Maronite militia and their Muslim counterparts could not work out their differences on power-sharing.

The Lebanese conflict came to an end only when regional and international factors converged and brought pressure to bear on the warring factions. After more than four decades of political conflict, which culminated in a bloody civil war that took more than 150,000 lives plus virtually destroyed the country's infrastructure and institutions, in 1989 the Taif Accord succeeded in devising an equal power-sharing formula between Muslim and Christian communities. The establishment of political equity between the Muslims and Christians has resolved one of the main conflicts stemming from the distribution of power.

The PSP views the Taif Accord as an essential mechanism to pacify the polity and reconstruct the democratic process. But the party's pursuit of its original objectives of secularization and democratization depend on its commitment to their realization. The PSP record during years between 1978 and 1996 does not look promising in this respect. Today the most important task that the PSP faces is restoring its secular political path, and its future role lies in fulfilling that goal successfully. If the PSP does not succeed in regaining its secular path, it will be just one more sectarian party among many others. Henceforth its political role can contribute to the consolidation of the new sectarian political system (Taif) rather than help in bringing about the secularization and the democratization of the political process.

The main lesson that we can draw from party experiences between 1949 and 1996 is that the PSP succumbed to the social and political pressures that typically confront secular parties in sectarian societies. This problem became more evident under the leadership of Walid Jumblatt, whose personal political choices responded positively to the dynamics of the sectarian stimulus emanating from the social structure. This contributed to the faltering of the PSP as a secular project. Thus in order to restore its founder's vision for a democratic, independent, secular, and just Lebanon, the PSP requires not only an overhaul and critical assessment of its past experiences, but it also requires meaningful changes in the social and political environment within which it operates. Such an objective can be fulfilled only if the political and social structures that have constrained the party are relaxed and secular democratic principles become the only rule of the political game. Such a measure could be a step toward the democratization of the social structure, which itself requires that two things be accomplished: sectarian/regional socioeconomic disparities are reduced; and rational-social values are injected into society by designing public policies to do so. Such policies would include a unified reading of the history of Lebanon and elimination of the sectarian personal status laws, or, at least, introducing "parallel" secular personal status laws.

But we cannot construct a theory about political parties in sectarian or multiethnic societies by devising what ought to be done to make their behavior conducive to democratic stability. Rather, our task is to identify the constraints under which parties operate and how these constraints shape political outcomes. In this context rational behavior, given structural constraints, does not lead to the wanted results (say, democracy). With actors constrained to take care of themselves, no one can take care of the democratic system. In other words, political parties, borrowing Kenneth Waltz's analogy on states' behavior, live in an anarchic environment where they act in a self-help system where each is struggling for power and resources in order to sustain their own survival, and do not seek the survival of the democratic system.[10] The prospects for democracy and the formation of strong secular political parties are not very bright in societies punctuated by deep class and ethnic cleavages, particularly when both coincide.

Chapter Six

The Predicament of Lebanon's Political Parties

THIS CHAPTER SITUATES THE CASE OF THE PSP within the larger context of party politics and social conflicts in Lebanon. It demonstrates that the party's inability to grow as a secular project was not an exception but rather the rule. The structures of power and the sectarian political system have circumvented the efforts of two of the most important secular parties in the country, the Lebanese Communist Party (LCP) and the Syrian Social National Party (SSNP), to develop as cross-sectarian organizations.

The chapter also analyzes the menu of choices and alternatives available as well as the structural constraints that led the leaders of these two parties to participate in the civil war. This analysis will help us to discern and identify patterns of political behavior when actors face similar structural and political conditions. Consequently, the chapter presents a prognosis of the future of secular parties in the aftermath of the Taif Accord.

Finally, this chapter concludes with a discussion of Lebanon's sectarian political parties and the malaise that has swamped these parties prior to and after the Taif Accord.

The LCP and the SSNP, the two largest secular political groups in Lebanon, were on the fringes of the country's political life more than ever before. Both group's secular ideologies inhibited the spread of their power bases beyond limited sectors of the Christian community (particularly the Orthodox Christians), and the Shiite and Druze, and less with the Sunni and Maronite communities.

THE LEBANESE COMMUNIST PARTY (LCP) BETWEEN SECTARIAN POWER STRUCTURES AND SECTOPOLITICS

The latest conference of the LCP held in Beirut in June 1993 reflected the impact of social and political structures on the party's sectarian composition: 69 percent of the conference delegates were Muslims; only 31 percent were Christians; and the Maronite delegates did not constitute more than 10 percent of the total number.[1] This fact suggests that the Communist Party, like the PSP, failed to attract wide support from the dominant Maronite status group. In contrast, the Shiite—the lowest-status group—constituted 41 percent of the delegates.[2] (See figure 6.1). This finding offers yet another proof to the argument that underpins this research.

Ghasan Rifai, the political bureau member of LCP, explained that the Christian Maronites low representation within LCP ranks can be attributed to Lebanon's structure of power and its corresponding sectarian system of political represention.[3] Rifai argues that prior to the establishment of the 1943 sectarian system, the Maronite membership within the LCP was relatively higher. He contends that that fact demonstrates that prior to 1943, sectarian representation had not yet been transformed into sectarian interests. Rifai's analysis suggests that despite the existence of sectarian representation in Lebanon since the latter part of the nineteenth century (see chapter 2), the interests of groups were not yet transformed from a primordial type of social solidarity to a rational type underpinned by clearer political and economic interests. Thus social groups in the post-1943 period began relating to their sect's political representatives as articulators of their interests and defenders of those interests versus the other sects. Rifai explains that the number of Maronite members during the first two decades after the inception of LCP (1920s and 1930s) was proportionally higher than in the post-1943 period. He attributed this decline to the transformation of sectarianism into political and status interests (what I called sectopolitics), that impeded LCP organizational efforts within the Maronite community.[4]

Rifai revealed that the LCP started recognizing the low representation of the dominant Maronite status group only after the second party conference of 1968. Yet only in the 1980s did this notion develop into

Figure 6.1 LCP sectarian composition in 1994

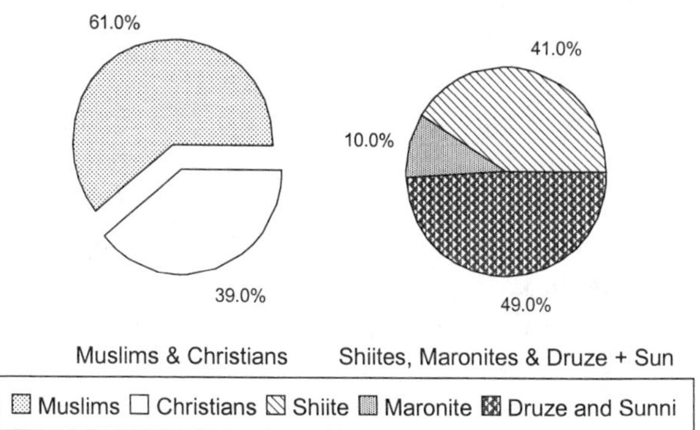

a coherent analysis similar to the one he offered. In other words, according to Rifai, the LCP did not fully appreciate the damaging affects of the sectarian power structures and sectopolitics on secular political parties until after the civil war of 1975, when the sectarian polarization brought to the surface the latent political power of sectarianism.

This lack of appreciation of the sectarian question led the LCP to commit grave political mistakes, such as its unconditional alliance with the PLO and other regional forces, which undermined its position within the ranks of the Christian community, particularly the Maronites. The LCP did not draw the necessary balance between a policy that accommodated the Lebanese power structures and the party's national democratic liberation goals. This failure, in my opinion, undermined the LCP's position not only within the Maronite community but also within the ranks of other sects (such as the Shiites), particularly after the dynamics of sectopolitics led to the emergence of sectarian political parties.

THE LCP POLITICAL BEHAVIOR

Since its inception in the 1920s as part of the Syrian Communist Party,[5] the LCP has been inclined to reform the political system by peaceful democratic means, a position that the party maintained even during the party's struggle for national independence from France. The party's commitment to reform did not, however, endear the LCP to the Maronite community at large, which perceived the party as a threat to its vital interests.

Examining the historical trajectory of the LCP particularly since the early 1970s is quite important for the study of its political behavior. In its 1973 conference, the LCP developed a concept of socialism within the context of democratic pluralism based on a multiparty system. This position coincided at the time with the PSP line, and in fact it formed the political basis for their future alliance. However, the adoption of a multiparty system of democracy did not insulate the LCP from the revolutionary winds that started blowing from different directions—particularly the escalation of the Arab-Israeli conflict since the 1967 war, which coincided with a growing socioeconomic crisis at home. Such conditions led to a radicalization within the party as members were exposed to a polarized social environment punctuated by a growing social crisis. (For examples, rates of unemployment reached 20 percent during that phase.)

Given the lack of progress on the reform front, the emergence of the "new left" with its revolutionary slogans and the presence of the Palestinian armed resistance influenced the party's rank and file. LCP members became increasingly socialized into a new radical political discourse. LCP cadres in the universities, high schools, factories, farms, and neighborhood organizations became increasingly challenged by the emerging radical left (such as the Organization of Communist Work, and the Socialist Work Party) on one side, and by the intransigent antireform extreme right on the other. In an interview with Kareem Mroueh, a political bureau member of the LCP, he emphasized that 1968 constituted a watershed in terms of the party's radical position against the state. He revealed that the polarized political environment of the late 1960s did have an impact on party policies, one of which was the unconditional support of the armed Palestinian presence. Hence the LCP, he concludes, contributed to the political polarization process and thus to prepare the ground for the civil war.[6]

Mroueh's views coincide with that of the secretary general of the Organization of Communist Work, Muhsin Ibrahim, who assessed the significance of the 1968 events in a similar way. Ibrahim contends that the causes of the 1975 civil war were an outgrowth of the 1967 Arab defeat in their war with Israel. He explained that the Maronite political leaders interpreted the Arab defeat as the right moment to recuperate from the losses they suffered politically during the 1958 crisis. Ibrahim argues that the 1968 trilateral Maronite alliance—al-hilf al-thulathi: Chamoun, Jumayyel, and Eddeh—presented a counterreform movement against the Shihab regime at the domestic level; at the regional level, its goal was to rectify the foreign policy "bias" toward the Arab side.[7]

But why 1968? Two important development took place in that year: The trilateral alliance among Maronite leaders emerged and called for Lebanon's neutrality in the Arab-Israeli conflict and steadfastly opposed any political reform on the domestic front; also the Palestinian resistance emerged as a viable political and military force on the Lebanese scene. These two developments were on a collision course.

The first showdown was in April 1969, when leftist and PLO supporters clashed with police forces and rightist militias of the three Maronite leaders in different areas of Lebanon. These events were the first steps toward the 1975 civil war.

The logical outcome of these changes in the LCP political environment was a change in its leadership, which occurred in 1973, when George Hawi became assistant secretary-general and the man in charge of organization.[8] These two positions made Hawi the party's strongman. The ascendance of Hawi and his allies reflected the new mood in the country and ushered in a change in the party's political behavior. The old guard, which for years espoused the possibility of change within the system's constitutional framework, despite its "unjust rules," became outranked by a younger and a more aggressive generation that ascended to the leadership under an increasingly polarized polity.

Consequently, the party started courting the PLO and the radical left represented by the Organization of Communist Work. But the swing toward a military option did not take full shape until 1978, when the LCP adopted the slogan "Toward the Construction of a Fighting Communist Party." It is important to note that during 1975-1976, the LCP was neither militarily nor politically prepared for the civil war.[9] Preparing its machine for war took the party a few years and required organizational and political changes in its hierarchy.

The convergence of domestic and regional variables exacerbated the contradictions in Lebanon to the point that local actors became victims of their own "small decisions" where outcomes could be unwanted by most if not all of them.[10] Consequently the LCP's "democratic option" was gradually overtaken by a series of "small decisions" responding to environmental stimuli. Perhaps the first "small decision" came after 1968, when the party reformulated its position toward the Arab-Israeli conflict and the Palestinian question. Such a change was championed by the younger LCP generation led by Hawi, who in 1967 suggested the creation of a military committee within the party. It was rejected by the LCP leadership at that time. But in 1969 this committee, whose objective was to prepare the LCP to defend the homeland in case of Israeli military aggression, was created with Hawi as its leader.[11] That same year fifty members of the LCP received military training.[12]

By 1973, when clashes between the PLO and the Lebanese army took place, LCP members started seeking arms from the PLO, particularly in Sidon and Beirut.[13] The party was sliding into the civil war, and gradually its "democratic option" for change was becoming obsolete. Yet the party did not abandon its official line until the late 1970s (i.e., a few years after the war officially began on April 13, 1975.

THE LCP AND THE 1975 CIVIL WAR AND ITS AFTERMATH

When the bus incident[14] of Ain al Rumena occurred on April 13, 1975, the Palestinian resistance decided to retaliate against some Christian sectors there and in Ashrafieh. This exacerbated an already tense situation. The LCP leadership declared as its political slogan the "political isolation" of the Kataib Party, the presumed perpetrator of the bus incident and the main conservative force against any political reform in Lebanon. According to Hawi, the decision to isolate the Kataib was taken by the LCP in order to avoid further military confrontations.[15] But as the events have shown us, the isolation of the Kataib became an instrument of sectopolitical polarization, particularly when the Muslim elite picked up the slogan. Consequently, isolating the Kataib became tantamount to isolating the Christian community at large. Hence instead of avoiding the military showdown, the isolation policy contributed to it and also led to the LCP's own isolation within the Maronite community. In brief, the LCP tactic proved to be a strategic error because it consolidated Kataib power within the Christian Maronite community and failed to prevent sectopolitical polarization and civil strife.

Reflecting on the causes of the civil war, Hawi said that he, Kamal Jumblatt, and Muhsin Ibrahim assumed that they were in full control of the political game and superimposed their desires over the existing political realities. Hawi added that the civil war experience demonstrated that the correlation of forces is always in favor of the stronger allies; consequently, the interests of those who are stronger supercede those of weaker allies.[16] In this sense the LNM misread the interests of its international allies (Soviet Union) and regional allies (PLO) which contributed to its own defeat. LNM international and regional allies eventually held their compromises at the LNM's expense. In this manner the LNM misperceived the international and regional configurations of power and their dynamic interplay in the country's scene.

Since 1982 the LCP has been engaged in an internal debate about the party's political orientations, alliances, political conduct during the civil war, and strategies. For our purpose, what is most relevant is the party's reevaluation of its course of action during the civil war. Two main points of view emerged. According to one group, the party ought to critique its political behavior during the civil war, particularly its contribution to the sectopolitical conflict. This group claims that the party's alliance with the Muslim political elite and the PLO was a historical mistake that caused the party to drift away from its secular goals and eroded its standing within the Christian community. A good number of those who held this view left the party in the early 1980s.[17]

The other point of view, which prevailed within the party, argued that withdrawing the party from the struggle against the Maronite Christian militia would have removed it from the national struggle against Western imperialism and its local clients.[18] This view was underpinned by the party's drive to change the balance of power in Lebanon in its favor, particularly since the LCP, like its ally the PSP, was frustrated by the dominant elite's resistance to political reform.[19] In the 1990s, echoes of the first view resurfaced again when Saadala Mazraani, an LCP political bureau member, in an interview conducted by *al-Nahar* daily on April 13, 1995, contended that the unconditional alliance with the PLO was a mistake that exacerbated the political contradictions in the country and certainly contributed to the civil war.

Inadvertently, however, the LCP became entangled in sectopolitics. It struggled to maintain its distinct secular position, but, as party officials acknowledged much later, it was not very successful in this respect, due to the polarized nature of the political environment.[20] The polity polarized the party members, who in turn became influenced by the dynamics of the war then raging. This was evident since 1968, culminating in 1978 when the party adopted the slogan "For the Construction of a Fighting Party," which reflected the mood within the LCP rank and file, particularly the young cadres.[21] In hindsight, it is not difficult to conceive how the Shiite or other LCP Muslim members would have reacted if the party had chosen to withdraw from the civil war. My guess is that mass defections would have occurred, something that happened anyhow after 1983, when the LCP withdrew from the south of Lebanon under military pressure from the Party of God and the Amal Movement.

The LCP leadership was certainly under enormous pressure to stay engaged in the war not only from its allies but also from within its own ranks. The party's political behavior was underlined by the following factors. One was the party's belief that the Muslim demand for the redistribution of political power and resources was a just cause that could serve the democratization of social relations in the country. (In chapter 1 I referred to other cases in which leftist parties followed similar paths in siding with subordinate ethnic groups).

Such thinking was reinforced by the support that the Maronite militia received from Israel and other Western nations, which tied the domestic power struggle with Cold War politics and alignments. As some party officials[22] later recognized, the Cold War thinking that dominated the party obscured the LCP vision about the inner dynamics of the civil war and contributed to its failure to pull the party out of the sectopolitical quagmire. Even in the mid-1980s, however, when the LCP realized the dangerous ramifications of continuing the political conflict on the future of Lebanon as a viable sovereign state, it tried, but was unable to withdraw from the conflict.

During that phase the LCP became a political target for different sectarian groups that it had antagonized earlier. Many of its most prominent leaders and intellectuals were killed between 1984 and 1990, and party properties were subject to military attacks. Thus, the LCP became drawn into a war-system and its anarchic rule, where self-help and self-preservation became the only ordering principles.

A third element was the LCP leaders' underestimation of the latent force of sectarianism that lent itself to political mobilization (i.e., becoming sectopolitics) at the disposal of sectarian parties. These factors intersected with the research findings on the PSP. As a result, it is possible to make generalizations regarding a certain pattern of behavior between secular political parties.

At another level, the LCP is yet to recover the significant political ground it lost to other sectarian political forces, such as Amal and the Party of God, which attracted some of its rank-and-file Shiite members. The Shiite community provided the party with about 40 percent[23] of its 7,000 members.[24] The LCP also has lost ground to the rightist Maronite militia. Although it has been weakened over the last ten years, the LCP still commands considerable support among intellectuals, university professors, artists, labor unions, women's groups, students, and others. Notwithstanding its acceptance of the Taif Accord, the LCP considers the power and institutional arrangements the accord produced to be a serious obstacle confronting political parties and the development of secular values in Lebanon. Consequently, I expect that the Taif regime will overwhelm the capabilities of secular political parties to act. Such parties may have to respond to the social stimuli generated by sectopolitics, in addition to the load that political parties normally assume in democratic systems.

Again the LCP failed in the 1996 parliamentary elections to get any of its candidates elected, although the party's candidates received 140,000 votes from a total of 1,100,000 voters, (i.e., about 13.5 percent of the national vote).[25] This fact reveals again that the electoral system in place inhibits the development of a party-system. It also reveals that the LCP commands a considerable support at the national level.

SOCIAL COMPOSITION OF THE SYRIAN SOCIAL NATIONAL PARTY (SSNP)

Another important secular force in Lebanon is the SSNP established in 1935 by Antoine Saadeh, a Lebanese middle-class Christian Orthodox. SSNP membership fluctuated over the years, but its main support base

Figure 6.2 SSNP's leadership sectarian composition, 1948-1958 and 1996

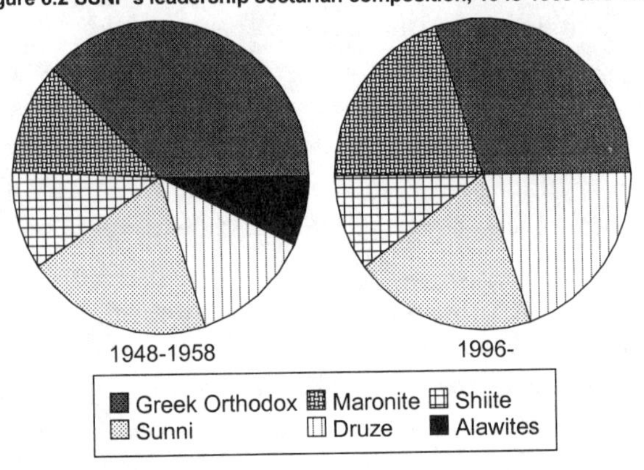

remained within the Christian Orthodox community. This was due to many historical and political factors, including the party's appeal to a Greater Syria, where there is a substantial concentration of Christian Orthodox.[26] The SSNP attracted supporters from the Shiite, Druze, and Sunni communities but few Maronites. In a study on the SSNP sectarian composition between 1948 and 1958, when sectopolitical polarization was not yet high, it was found that only eight out of seventy-one party leaders were Maronites, whereas twenty-six were Greek Orthodox; fourteen were Sunni, nine were Druze, seven were Shiites, and five were Alawites.[27] No evidence suggests that such representation was reversed in the following years. In the 1996 elections of the al Majlis al Ala—the party's executive committee—three were Christian Orthodox, two Christian Maronites, two Sunni, two Druze, one Shiite and one Christian Catholic.[28](See figure 6.2).

Thus the PSP, LCP, and SSNP shared a common characteristic: the conspicuously low representation of the dominant Maronite status group in their ranks. This fact supports my argument that social and political structures have influenced the sectarian makeup of Lebanon's main secular parties.

Regarding its past conduct, the SSNP tried two coup attempts, one in 1949 and the other in 1961. These attempts were motivated partially by the party's nationalistic zeal. Some argue that the SSNP links with British intelligence played an important role in designing and executing these unsuccessful coups.[29] Regardless of the motives, since then the party has reformed itself to accommodate the new political realities of Lebanon's consociational democracy. The fruits of these reforms came to bear in the late 1960s, when the SSNP started courting the Lebanese left to accept the interim reform program proposed by the PSP in 1975.

The party reevaluated its past policies, particularly its antagonistic position toward the Communist movement and the PSP. It is worth mentioning in this respect that the SSNP sided with President Chamoun during the 1958 crisis. This political shift removed the party from its peculiar position to the right of the political spectrum. In the early 1970s the party became part of the leftist coalition and an active member of the Lebanese National Movement, with the SSNP president becoming the LNM vice president. Thus, during the fifteen-years-long civil war, the party fought on the side of the left against the rightist forces, including the militia of President Chamoun's Liberal National Party, the SSNP's ex-ally.

Under the leadership of Inam Raed, the SSNP moved closer to the PSP, due to political affinities and to the rapport between Kamal Jumblatt and Raed.[30] This coalition reinforced the party's political choices and position toward political reform. The SSNP decision to participate in the war was affected by a number of factors, including the party's coalition with Jumblatt and the LNM, which underscored SSNP's political reorientation toward the left and the Palestinian resistance since the late 1960s. In the late 1960s and early 1970s, SSNP coalition with the leftist parties made its members targets of harassment and murder by rightist militias in areas dominated by the Kataib Party, their staunchest foe.[31] Those attacks intensified by the mid-1970s, forcing the SSNP leaders to withdraw party members from these areas and join the war in earnest.[32]

The SSNP's previous predisposition against the democratic process cannot solely explain the party's decision to join the war, because since the failed coup of 1961, the party revised its line closer to that of the PSP and LCP. Consequently, the SSNP accepted the LNM's "Interim Reform Program," which called for a peaceful democratic change within the constitutional framework of Lebanon.[33] In this sense therefore, by the early 1970s the SSNP seemingly abandoned its past "erratic" behavior.

Then why did the SSNP and its allies abandon their declared commitment to a democratic option? Three factors can explain the shift in the SSNP stance: a rigid power structure, which excluded the main secular forces from the political process (the LCP, SSNP, and the PSP to a lesser degree); the intransigent position of the Maronite political elite which refused to accept any reform in the distribution of power; and the spillover effects of the regional and international Cold War struggle that came into play with the internal contradiction. This last factor reduced further the choices available and influenced the actors' incentives and increased the constraints on political action. The armed presence of the PLO and its alliance with the SSNP and its allies made the military option a risk worth taking. It is safe to conclude that given the social and political structures and the historical circumstances under which those parties operated, they could not have behaved differently, particularly because they were only part of a political game in which they did not command full control.

Yet despite the concerted efforts of the LNM, its parties sank into a sectopolitical swamp. In fact, they fatally underestimated the depth of sectarianism in the psyche of the Lebanese masses and the pivotal role of sectopolitics. Of course, there are a number of other contributing factors that led to the marginalization of the secular parties, most important the assassination of Kamal Jumblatt and Syria's policies toward Lebanon. Both factors inhibited the LNM's development; the loss of Jumblatt deprived the LNM of its most important leader, and the Syrian regime weakened and co-opted the LNM's parties. In the late 1980s the SSNP divided into two main factions, one led by Inam Raed and the other by Issam Maheyri. Syria's role in this split is evident, according to the informants and officials that were interviewed. The Maheyri faction known as the SSNP-Tawaree (SSNP-Emergency), the closest to Syria, won five seats in the 1996 parliamentary election while the Raed faction failed to win any seat.

However, the political decay of these parties and the conspicuous absence of a strong alternative secular political group reveal how hostile the sociopolitical environment was to secular values and norms. The social environment can be characterized as being manipulated by a political system that could reproduce itself by a precarious process of sectarian balancing. When the social and political contradictions disturbed its balance, a volcano erupted—the 1975 civil war—which came as a surprise to the leaders of those parties.[34]

The Lebanese case raises serious doubts about the possibility of building effective popular secular political parties in severely divided societies, because secular parties are largely influenced and shaped by the modes of struggle between the different ethnic or religious groups.[35] If confronted by rigid power structures and political institutions favoring one group over others, secular political parties face three difficult choices. They may adopt the claims of the underprivileged groups, thus alienating members of the dominant ethnic group and becoming part of the ethnic conflict. They may side with the dominant group, henceforth subjecting themselves to the wrath of the subordinate group. Finally, they may take a neutral position, situating themselves on the fringe of the political game. These three scenarios illustrate the predicament of secular parties in multiethnic societies. In Lebanon, most secular parties supported the Muslim demand for a just and equitable distribution of political power and resources. This political choice of the LNM alienated a good number of Maronite Christians.

During the 1976 to 1989 phase, the dynamics of the conflict underpinned by sectarian atrocities committed by sectarian groups gradually rendered the secular parties ineffective. In their place arose a new genre of political groups predominantly sectarian in their social base and with a sectopolitical ideologies. Thus despite the fact the secular parties positioned themselves on the Muslim side, they were overtaken by sectarian groups. In retrospect, perhaps the alliance between the left and the Muslim elite inadvertently contributed to such an outcome by releasing the dormant sectarian genie from its bottle, rejuvenating the monster of sectopolitics, and also unleashing other archaic social values. Now, after the storm and after the dust of war has settled, we can analyze events in retrospect. The following general characteristics of the actors involved in the "human drama" of Lebanon may provide some guidelines of topics for future research on the prospects of democratization in severely divided multiethnic or sectarian societies:

- Actors were subject to pressures stemming from institutional and social power arrangements and the lack of progress on political reform.
- Actors underestimated the latent force of sectarianism and the polarizing affects of sectopolitics.
- They were not totally committed to democracy yet they abided by its rules under certain conditions.
- They valued political change more than democracy and were willing to take risks.

- Alliances were made with regional and international forces (PLO, the Soviet Union).
- The regional and international dimensions of the armed conflict and its inner dynamic reduced the choices available to actors.[36]

My investigation validated these observations. My main finding is that political behavior is, in the final analysis, a complex phenomenon informed by multiple variables: social and institutional arrangements (rules of the game), the actors' own calculations, alliances, and political predispositions.

SECTARIAN POLITICAL PARTIES: DYNAMICS BETWEEN SOCIAL STRUCTURES AND AGENCIES

Now a general description of the main sectarian groups in Lebanon, namely the Kataib Party, the Lebanese Forces, the Amal Movement, and the Party of God, is in order.

Sectarian parties—or sectopolitical parties—are here defined as those groups that recruit mainly from one sect or religion. Furthermore, unlike secular political parties, these groups do not even intend to establish mass multisectarian political parties.

Despite the fact that sectarian political parties gained significant ground in the years between 1976 and 1997, they also have been confronted by a series of problems stemming from intrasectarian power struggles. The intrasectarian rivalries reveal the existence of social forces such as regionalism that did not affect secular parties in the same way. Regionalism is a form of social solidarity based on place of birth and sense of belonging to a specific region. It is a kind of group association that has been part of Lebanon's social fabric and important in the making of its body politics. Regional loyalties come as part of other loyalties, such as those to a sect or to a family or clan.[37]

Regional loyalties per se did not influence secular parties (with the exception of the PSP after 1977), because these parties were essentially struggling against the existing social and political structures, hence were able to minimize the effects of regionalism. Regional loyalties became more salient in parties that were constructed along the traditional lines of power within the sect. Thus the sect's inner power structures, with its contradictions, become part and parcel of the sect party. This became apparent when one political force within the sect attempted to subsume the representation of the entire sect. A case in point was the Kataib and then the Lebanese Forces.

This analytical framework allows us to understand the conflicts within the LF and between the LF and the Kataib and General Michel Oun. Similarly, the same framework can help in analyzing the conflict between the Party of God and the Amal Movement.

It is important to emphasize that after Kamal Jumblatt's death, the PSP became enmeshed with the contradictions stemming from the inner power structures of the Druze community, particularly the social divides between the Druze of the Shouf and those of Aley and the Maten,[38] only when the PSP was totally transformed into a sectarian party and claimed to represent the Druze.

Although Kamal Jumblatt was sensitive to Druze regional power structures, there is no evidence that these sensitivities found their way into the PSP during his leadership. Although he manipulated these structures and put them to serve the PSP, particularly during election periods, he tried to keep the PSP out of the orbit of Druze politics and used his Druze base as a springboard to national and secular politics. That explains why Kamal Jumblatt was eager to keep the leadership of the PSP multisectarian and why the PSP earnestly tried to expand its power base beyond the Druze community.

Under Walid Jumblatt, who assumed the leadership when sectopolitical polarization was gaining momentum, the PSP became more in tune with the sectarian impulses. Since 1978, the composition of the PSP leadership and middle-ranking officers started to reflect regional considerations peculiar to the Druze community. Conflicts within the PSP ranks did occur between partisans from the Shouf and those from Aley regions on several occasions between 1984 and 1989, but they remained under control and never approximated the intensity reached by the other intersectarian conflicts in the 1980s.

Intrasectarian rivalries in Lebanon caused equal, if not more, death and destruction than intersectarian wars. Most students of the civil war, which focused on intersect violence, largely overlooked this fact. For example, the intra-Maronite fighting between the Kataib and the Lebanese Forces and the confrontations with the predominantly Maronite brigades of the fractured Lebanese army caused more than 50 percent of the total fatalities suffered by the LF during the civil war.[39] The remaining casualties fell in confrontations with the leftist-PLO alliance. Furthermore, the global costs of the Oun-LF two-year war amounted to $2 billion whereas the total costs of the fourteen years of civil war were about $6 billion.[40]

Similarly, the Shiite power struggle between the Party of God and Amal Movement caused the most fatalities among both groups militants. These two examples illustrate some of the dilemmas of sectopolitical parties in Lebanon and highlight another aspect of the social structure that came to influence sectarian parties, namely regionalism and rural/urban divides. These cleavages could help us explain some of the root causes of the intrasectarian conflicts that took place throughout the 1980s and early 1990s. Due to group fragmentation, these conflicts made even the task of constructing a political system based on sectarian parties formidable. Sectarian political parties lacked enough cohesion to sustain any political system, let alone a consociational democracy.

A few years before the 1975 civil war, the Lebanese sociologist Samir Khalaf argued that the norms of the Lebanese society, such as kinship, familism, personalism, regionalism, patron-client networks, and their intersection with sectarianism, would not be cured solely by the abolishment of sectopolitics (i.e., political representation based on sect). Khalaf emphasized that informal features (family ties, regionalism, and other ascriptive relations) of the social structure would hinder the emergence of a democratic order.[41] Certainly my discussion partially supports Khalaf's contention, particularly in respect to the tenacity of sectarianism and other "primordial" values in the Lebanese society when reinforced by the political regimes of 1943 and the Taif Accord of 1989 respectively.

I also think, however, that regionalism emerged as an aspect of the Lebanese conflict for two main causes. One is the survival of traditional ascriptive values within the society despite more than a century of capitalist development. This condition is due to the mode of Lebanon's capitalist development where precapitalist values and social structures became enmeshed with capitalist ones. Solidarities based on kinship and/or belonging to a village remained important sources of identity and constituted bases for sociopolitical solidarities within the sects.[42] Second, and as a consequence of the first reason, the dynamics of the conflict have even reversed some secularizing trends that existed prior to the 1975 war, and thus have reinforced primordial solidarities. I explain these two observations in the rest of this chapter.

THE KATAIB, THE LEBANESE FORCES, AND THE OUN PHENOMENA

The Kataib Party, founded in 1936 by Pierre Jumayyel, played a major role in Lebanon's politics for most of this century. A predominantly middle-class Maronite party, the Kataib, became one of the main defenders of the political system in Lebanon and a strong ally of the bourgeoisie, particularly its Maronite sector. Since its inception the party passed through several stages that allowed it to become a reliable political and military force upon which the Maronite bourgeoisie relied in moments of crisis. The first test for the Kataib was in 1958, when it mobilized a substantial number of its militants to defend the regime of Camille Chamoun. More than a decade later, in 1969, the Kataib demonstrated again its military capacities during confrontations with leftist parties and the Palestinian guerrillas. Since then the party has been gradually transformed into an impressive military machine. Between 1976 and 1980 the party's military became part of an umbrella organization called the Lebanese Forces, which included other small Maronite parties, such as the National Liberal Party (headed by Camille Chamoun) and the Front of Cedars' Guards. In 1980 the Lebanese Forces became a unified military structure under Bashir Jumayyel after he succeeded in defeating the National Liberal Party's militia, which opposed the Kataib hegemony.

Between the years 1980 and 1982, the LF succeeded in establishing its political autonomy from the Kataib and in effect became the most decisive political force within the Maronite community under Bashir Jumayyel, Pierre Jumayyel's younger son. The emergence of the LF as a political power caused a rupture in the power structure that reached a crisis point after the death of Bashir and Pierre Jumayyel respectively. During their leadership both had helped to keep a lid on the crisis.

THE KATAIB AND THE CIVIL WAR

The Kataib entered the civil war, abandoning the democratic framework for gun politics as the leader of the Christian Maronite forces against the LNM-PLO alliance. Since it began, the Kataib Party has been inspired by the models of European fascist parties; hence it had a strong militaristic underpinning.[43] This ideological predisposition underscored the party's political behavior toward the opposition as early as

1949, when the Kataib confronted SSNP recruiters in the Joumaizeh area, a predominantly Christian neighborhood in Beirut. In 1949, Kataib members attacked the SSNP printing press and succeeded in destroying it in an attempt to halt the SSNP recruitment efforts within the Christian community. Paradoxically, the battle led to the ban of SSNP. The Kataib outlaw was only perfunctory and within a few weeks it was recognized by the government as Hizb al Itihad al Lubnani (the Party of Lebanese Unity).

This example shows that the Kataib was designed as a defender of the political system and protector of the prevailing power structure. Such a role was legitimated by the party's ideology, which claimed the uniqueness of the Lebanese Christians within a predominantly Muslim Arab environs; according to the party, Lebanon's power structures, role, and foreign policy always should reflect such uniqueness. In effect, the Kataib was struggling to preserve and legitimate the hegemony of the Maronite bourgeoisie within the power structure; in turn, this "uniqueness" of Lebanon was defined in terms of the hegemonic position of the Maronite elite.

The emergence of the Arab national movement during the 1950s alarmed the Kataib, especially after the Muslim started courting this movement. During the 1958 crisis, the Kataib emerged as a vital force for the survival of the regime, especially after the army failed to render support to Chamoun's ambition for a second presidential term. The multisectarian composition of the army made it difficult to maintain its unity should it combat a predominantly Muslim opposition. The 1958 events alarmed the Maronite elite, and the Kataib learned that the Maronite hegemony could not be protected by the state's army. Thus, the Kataib paramilitary groups were to be prepared as a strategic reserve that this elite might need, particularly in a regional environment where Cold War polarization was increasingly becoming the order of the day, with all its domestic ramifications.

The Kataib began acquiring heavy weapons after 1969 and increased after the PLO-military clashes of 1973.[44] Kareem Pakradouni, political bureau member of the Kataib and the current secretary-general of the party, revealed that during the 1973 clashes, President Sleiman Franjieh gave notice to Pierre Jumayyel that "the Lebanese army cannot perform its functions, thus this function is left to the Kataib."[45] After that, according to Pakradouni, the shipments of heavy armaments began arriving to the party.

Thus the Kataib's movement toward the war option was incremental and gradual, not a decision taken on the spur of the moment. Rather, the Kataib Party had an ideological predisposition, as it thought of itself as a defender of the prevailing power structures the war option was a logical one to assume. What underscored this option was the Kataib leadership's belief that any reform of the political system would open a Pandora's box that might lead to a Muslim president. According to Pakradouni, this fear has underpinned the Kataib leaders' position toward political reform from 1936 to 1989, when the party changed course.[46] Pierre Jumayyel rejected any attempt to abolish the sectarian system of political representation because he thought doing so might undermine the favored Maronite elite's hegemonic position.[47]

Hence, according to Pakradouni, Rogis Dib, and other informants, as long ago as 1969 and 1973; the Kataib decided to face any challenge to the established regime by force, if necessary. Thus the Kataib's position against political reform and its militaristic inclination and tradition put the party on an inevitable collision course with the LNM and the PLO. Perhaps the best illustration of the dynamics that led to the civil war is the one presented by Muhsin Ibrahim, one of the main leaders at that time. During an interview he said:

> The basic problem in Lebanon has been the divides between the Muslim and Christian Maronite communities over the issue of pan-Arabism, especially after the Arab defeat in the 1967 war with Israel. Consequently, two diametrically opposed positions emerged: one that called for a Lebanon unconditionally allied with the PLO and tied in with the Arab-Israeli conflict, and the other championed by the Kataib, calling for the isolation of Lebanon from this conflict and the prohibition of the PLO operations from Lebanese territory. These two positions were in effect "two war programs" that started taking institutional forms (by the processes of armament, military training, and consequently creating militias) after the bloody demonstrations of April 1969.[48]

Ibrahim acknowledged that he championed the first position. His view resonates with that of Pakradouni, who presented a similar account of the events leading up to the civil war.

Therefore, the Kataib was committed to an uncompromising position against any political reform and prevented any alterations in Lebanon's internal balance of power that might affect the distribution of political power. Thus, the party saw the PLO's armed presence and its alliance with the Muslim community as a direct threat to the Maronite elite's position. The Kataib decided to face the threat head on by building its military apparatus and by striking alliances with Israel and other regional and international forces.

The emergence of the two uncompromising "war programs" led to the faltering of the consociational arrangement, which was essentially based on a compromise. The lack of compromising leaders, save the efforts of Kamal Jumblatt, led to a deepening of the sectarian divide in a country that must, due to its multiconfessional composition, be based on compromises, if democracy is the desired objective.[49] Of course, democracy was subsumed by the power struggle between the opposing political groups and many opportunities for compromise were lost.[50]

THE KATAIB AND THE CRISIS OF POWER

Between 1985 and 1997 the party suffered constant infighting between the old guard and the younger generation, which cost it dearly in terms of political credibility and prestige within the Christian Maronite community. The decline of the Kataib was precipitated by a number of factors, primarily the party's organizational rigidity, which did not give enough space for the young and ambitious militia leaders who emerged during the civil war.[51] As the party was unable to adapt to the new environment generated by the dynamics of conflict, young militia leaders turned to the Lebanese Forces, the umbrella military organization of the rightist alliance, and gradually the Lebanese Forces supplanted the Kataib and replaced it as the "monolithic" voice representing the Christians.[52]

Kareem Pakradouni attributed the Kataib crisis to three other factors that are intrinsic to the party's peculiarity: The first factor is the struggle between different groups within and without the party to control it, which ensued after the death of Pierre Jumayyel, the party's founder and leader. Those contending forces believe that he who controls the Kataib controls the Christian community, due to its core position within the structure of political power. The Kataib was strong enough organizationally to become a mass party. Yet struggles between Amin Jumayyel and Samir Jaja over the party's presidency weakened its standing within the Christian community.

The second factor was the inability of George Saadeh, Pierre Jumayyel's successor and current party president, to gain the political support of the different factions within the party, particularly that of the faction led by Amin Jumayyel.

The third factor is that the Kataib produced two presidents including Amin Jumayyel, who finished a six-year term. Although Jumayyel, according to Pakradouni, did not govern with the mandate and program of the Kataib, according to laypeople he was a Kataib symbol. Consequently the party paid for the failures of Jumayyel's presidency, which was characterized by inefficiency, widespread corruption, and lack of leadership, in popular support and prestige.

Finally, Pakradouni concluded that the Kataib crisis stems from what he termed as the "crisis of achieving its grand objectives." He explains that since its inception in 1936, the Kataib claimed that Lebanon is an end in itself, one worth struggling for against the incorporation into the schemes of Arab unity. But now that the Taif Accord has clearly defined Lebanon as a sovereign land, the main objective of the party has been achieved. Its second main objective has been the preservation of a liberal democratic system, which all parties now accept as the framework of modern Lebanon. He added that another party objective was to find a peaceful solution to the Arab-Israeli conflict; with the arrival of the peace process, this goal is almost achieved. Finally, the Kataib's long-standing position against pan-Arabism was changed in favor of an acceptance of it, Pakradouni concluded. In essence, Pakradouni believes the Kataib lost its raison d'être; it lost its ability to differentiate itself from other political groups in Lebanon. Thus, he concluded, the party needs urgently a new identity and political orientation.

Defections and splits characterized the post-1984 phase, when a good number of Kataib members defected to the Lebanese Forces (outlawed in 1994) or simply took a neutral position. The major cause of the Kataib crisis was a lack of political direction after the party lost its founder and leader, Pierre Jumayyel, in 1984. No other leader has been acceptable to the party rank and file. Pierre Jumayyel's death came at a time of increased challenges to the party legitimacy within the Maronite community. By the mid-1980s, Samir Jaja and Elie Hubaika (both of whom joined the Kataib in the early 1970s) were ready to jump into the power vacuum. As a result, a power struggle ensued between the "legitimate heir," Amin Jumayyel, and the new leaders of the Lebanese Forces, who were trying to take over the party leadership in an attempt to terminate the dual authority between the LF and the Kataib.

Much of the intrasectarian conflict revolved around the power arrangements and distribution of resources. According to Rogis Dib, the secretary-general of the Kataib (1989-1992), the conflicts within the LF and between it and the Kataib were primarily between the underprivileged and newly displaced Maronites with what he called the "establishment." In Dib's opinion, the "establishment" consists of the old guard of the Kataib and their associates within the LF, such as Fuad abu Nader, who assumed the LF leadership (1982-1985) after Bashir Jumayyel. Abu Nader, a relative of the Jumayyel family, was ousted in 1985 by an alliance between factions of Hubeika and Jaja.

The LF political base of support is predominantly from the periphery (rural Maronite) areas. Paradoxically, in 1975, the Kataib also drew its main support from the new Maronite migrants to the cities.[53] John Entelis's study of the Kataib supports this fact.[54] Although the LF's initial power base was drawn from the same pool of rural migrants, as the war progressed supporters shifted to the thousands of Christians refugees who escaped Muslim and Christian areas that were outside the rightist militia territorial domain. After 1975 those refugees consequently became the backbone of the LF, particularly after the 1978 Ihdin massacre in the north of Lebanon, in which Tony Franjieh, son of president Sleiman Franjieh, and his family were killed by members of the LF.

In the wake of this massacre, reprisals were taken by the Franjieh clan against the Kataib and LF supporters in Zgharta and its environs in north Lebanon. Hundreds escaped these regions, later forming the core of the LF under the leadership of Jaja, who came from Bshari (which is near Zgharta). By then the profile of a typical LF member contrasted sharply with the relatively settled "urbanite" Kataib member. The typical LF member carries cultural baggage inclined more toward vengeance and violence attributed to the conditions that led to his or her displacement.[55]

By the mid-1980s, the LF was drawing its members predominantly from the young population (average age twenty to thirty); about 70 percent were from rural areas (provinces rather than big cities); and most were displaced and without jobs. The older veteran members of the Kataib typically were about thirty years and older, lower middle class, from Mount Lebanon[56] (not from the rural north or south), and most likely lived in a major city prior to the 1975 war.

Most of the LF leaders were of lower-class to lower-middle-class origins.[57] The Kataib leaders were drawn from professionals of middle class to upper-income groups.[58] These social differences between the two organizations help to explain some of the root causes that led to the schisms between them, ending in a complete divorce in 1993. The Lebanese government outlawed the LF after its leader, Samir Jaja, and some of his followers were accused of a series of bombings that rocked Beirut in 1994. As of this writing Jaja is serving a jail sentence.

The Kataib Party, on its part, lost its standing as "the Maronite party," and its image, prestige, and power have diminished significantly since 1984. The question that begs for an answer is how effective the Kataib will be in wake of these political and organizational changes.

The political decay of the Kataib is beyond repair due to a number of factors, of which I will mention only two. First, the social and political changes in the Maronite community that took place in the last two decades caught up with the party. An overhaul of party structures was required to adapt to these changes, which the current leadership was unwilling to do, because that could lead to their demotion and the ascendance of the LF members who enjoy a wide support within the Kataib rank and file.[59] Second, both the Kataib and the LF face a common challenger, the populist leader Michel Oun, who commands strong support among the Maronite and other communities. Oun became prime minister for about two years after Amin Jumayyel's presidential term ended in 1988. Oun, the ex-commander of the Lebanese Army, had a new leadership style, charisma, and nationalist slogans against the Syrians, Israelis, and the militia rule, which attracted wide support from different sects.

In the 1996 parliamentary elections, the Kataib failed to get any of its candidates elected, which added insult to injury, exacerbating the identity crisis of the party and further marginalizing its political role.

In conclusion, the crisis of the Kataib Party is not only organizational; it is also of political nature that concerns the soul of the party. The crisis stems from the inability of a conservative political force to adapt and develop in tune with the changes in the international political environment in the post–Cold War era and, more important, to adjust to the potent incorporating forces of global capitalism, which are changing the political economy of Lebanon and redefining its role and relationship with other regional actors, particularly Syria. The Kataib seems unable to adapt to the changes in its environment; as Samuel Huntington suggested, it lacked institutionalization in that the Kataib suffered from extreme factionalism after the death of its historical leader and was unable to adapt to the necessities of a new political economy.

THE GENERAL AND THE PROSPECTS FOR HIS MOVEMENT

General Michel Oun promised to open a new page in the history Lebanon based on national unity, which touched a chord that had long been overshadowed by sectopolitics. Perhaps what made Oun appealing is that he appeared on the scene when people were exhausted from the LF's militia rule and its bickering with the Kataib Party.[60]

The emergence of Oun and the support he commands suggests that he shifted the political power farther away from the Kataib, undermining its position in the power structure. On the other hand, Oun checked the rising star of the LF, leading to its delegitimization as the "sole" representative of the Christian Maronite community, which in turn raised serious doubts about who the "legitimate heir" of the Kataib might be.

In my opinion, Oun's popular movement put into question the credibility of both the Kataib and the Lebanese Forces and put them into a peripheral position in the emerging power structure in the Maronite community. Oun's political movement created a crack in the edifice of power and generated new key players within the Maronite community who are outside both the Kataib and the LF. In spite of its limited success in capitalizing on the popular support, Oun's influence is evident in his supporters' visible political activism.

According to the spokesperson of Oun's movement, Nadeem Ltaif, "in 1995 and 1996 the movement achieved important political victories in a number of key unions' elections such as: labor unions, student unions, engineers, lawyers, and medical doctors."[61] The main challenge that this group faces is how to organize and institutionalize its popular support and build a political party or any other form of collective action.

Currently Oun chairs *al-Moutamar al-Lubnani* (The National Free Wing). My impression is that the movement is highly centralized and all decisions are in the hands of its chairman. The dilemma facing the movement and the manner in which it is resolved will largely determine the group's future. The dilemma is how to accommodate Oun's populist appeal with the necessities of forming a political party with a clear political program that is committed to certain specific goals. Defining the movement's objectives may damage the loose alliance that is based on general slogans. That is to say, the main source of power of Oun's movement—its loose alliance based on nationalistic and populist slogans—is also its main weakness, particularly if it decides to transform itself into a political party.

Oun's movement is at a crossroads; he must decide either to build a national, secular political party—which could deny him significant support among the Christian community—or to concentrate on his Christian Maronite power base. I believe the latter is more likely in accord with the Taif sectarian arrangement and the nature of the group's ideological orientation. After all, Oun is the political product of a sectopolitical regime and his discourse thus far did not demonstrate any rapture with such a regime.

Regardless of Oun's future course of action, what is now certain is that he is a key player in any future power configuration. But, for now, and until a new balance is established and the Syrian veto against Oun is relaxed, the Maronite church will be the caretaker of the Maronite political representation.

The social sectors that supported Oun in his fight against the LF reveal that he represented a backlash against the "political ruralization" of the city. Under Jaja, the LF came to represent the Christian city dwellers of Asahrafieh, Jouneih, Maten, and Jubail, marking a political invasion by the peripheries.[62] Oun touched on a very sensitive nerve among many Christians when he promised to rid them of LF militia rule. In this sense, Oun's effort to oust the LF was perhaps the last attempt to reverse the political tide and recapture the initiative by the city elites, such as ex-president Amin Jumayyel and other traditional

Kataib leaders, who lost to Jaja and his LF forces. Now, with the dissolution of and the ban on the LF, the city elites seem to have won this round, at least for the moment.

Oun was overtaken by his own "nationalistic" discourse which underestimated the changes in the regional and international political environment which was inching toward peace. The Middle East peace process required the United States and other regional players to accommodate the Syrian interests in Lebanon, which Oun refused to do. Because he built his political image on the notion of fighting for the sovereignty of Lebanon, giving concessions in this area could have undermined his own position. Oun was removed from power by a military operation carried out by the Syrian army in 1991; since then he has lived in exile in France.

THE AMAL MOVEMENT AND THE PARTY OF GOD: UNEASY COEXISTENCE AND POWER STRUGGLE

Two main Shiite organizations vie for political power in Lebanon, the Amal Movement and the Party of God. Their competition for supremacy is also underpinned by regional, political, and ideological factors. Most Amal partisans are from the south of Lebanon, the stronghold of Amal leader Nabeeh Berri. In contrast, the Party of God commands more support in the Biqa' Valley, where its leadership wove a loose network of tribal, clan, and family relations.

Since the mid-1980s, Amal has been rocked by a number of political defections and splits, such as the one led by the Hassan Mousawi faction, which later joined the Party of God. Then came the split of Akel Hamieh, the head of Amal's security, who also joined the Party of God in 1987. Later three of the most powerful men in Amal, Akef Haidar, Mahmoud Dirani, and Hasan Hashim, also left the party after a dispute with Berri. The common denominator among these members of the Amal political bureau is that they are from the Biqa'/Hirmel region. Seemingly their regional background was one factor that led to their differences with the movement's leader. A good number of these men disputed Berri's policy toward south Lebanon and Israel. Most contested his call for the pacification of south Lebanon in an attempt to save it from Israel's military reprisals. Currently, most Amal Movement leaders are from south Lebanon.

Factional disputes within Amal and between Amal and the Party of God arise against the backdrop of other factors that influence intra-Shiite politics, such as the social differences between the Shiites of the south and those from the Hirmel and Biqa'.

The Shiite of the Biqa' believe the Shiites of the South are complacent and subservient, and lack the spirit of *assabiyya* (using Ibn Khaldun's term of strong solidarity and loyalty among clan members). In the Biqa' clan ties are still strong and acquired functional importance during the civil war due to economic necessities that generated clan insecurities.

In the South, however, clan loyalties dissipated due to the pattern of socioeconomic development, particularly the emigration of a significant part of its population, which started in the late 1940s. This emigration gradually changed the fortunes of tens of families and entire villages (e.g., Juayya, Harees, Nabatiya and Tyre) and introduced new elements into the social fabric, particularly reducing the social functions of the clan and the extended family. In contrast, the Biqa' population became influenced by the tide of emigration much later and continued to rely on agriculture and on employment in the army, police, and other state bureaucracies. Thus they could preserve some of their traditional clan values. The conflict between the two groups may have been partially due to Shiite regional differences, particularly their respective feelings of *assabiyya,* which provides to the group that sense of manhood and stamina to fight the "enemy." This *assabiyya* is set against a backdrop of the status differentiation between the two communities, which reinforces their social differences and conflicts.[63]

The two main Shiite parties also have different sources of support, which also divided their loyalties. The Party of God is linked with Iran, whereas Amal Movement is a very close ally of Syria. These alliances have also influenced the relationship between the two political parties and their behavior during and after the civil war.

The relationship between the two Shiite parties has been, for the most part, tense. In an effort to gain command of power in the Shiite community during the late 1980s, the two parties fought fierce battles in southern Lebanon and in the southern suburbs of Beirut, resulting in hundreds of injuries and deaths in addition to extensive property damage. Districts and even streets divided between supporters of each party. After reaching an understanding of the share each has in the Shiite power structure, the current relationship between the two parties is a "cold peace." Both have deputies in the country's parliament, elected in 1992 and 1996. The Party of God's share was eight representatives in 1992 and seven in 1996; Amal Movement had five in 1992 and increased its share to seven in 1996, and also gained the second most important position in government, the chairmanship of the parliament. This division of political power also reflects the support each group enjoys in its respective region.

In organizational structures, the Party of God has a centralized Leninist structure, particularly in its security and military arms. Its political bureau (Maglis-Siyasi) accommodates status, clan, and family ties within the Shiite community. The political bureau is appointed by the Shura (consultative) council—the highest authority—which is composed of seven members, including the secretary-general, the chairman of the political bureau, and the chairman of the executive council. The Shura Council is composed mainly of Shiite clerics.[64] The 20,000 Party of God members are drawn mainly from rural Shiite areas and are of lower- and middle-class origins.[65]

Since 1997 the Party of God has witnessed internal factionalism. A faction led by Subhi al-Tufaily-from Breital (near Baalbek in the Biqa') emerged, ushering in a new realignment in the party's regional structures. The causes of this conflict are several—one of which is that the party leaders from the south have gained more weight than those of the Biqa', one of the complaints of the Tufaily faction. Hassan Nassrallah, the party leader, is from the south, and other key positions in the political bureau and all but one in Majlis al-Shura are occupied by leaders from the south. Of course this is not to deny that other political factors came into play in this factional dispute which culminated in an armed conflict in January 1998, but to highlight the importance of regional cleavages in intrasectarian relations.[66]

The Amal Movement is less structured; although it has a political bureau, authority revolves around its leader. Personalism plays a more pronounced role in Amal than in the Party of God, the SSNP (in the post-Antoine Saadeh phase, because Saadeh's leadership was highly personalistic), and the LCP. Its structure comes closest to the PSP under the leadership of Walid Jumblatt.

The Party of God with its regional ties has become a key player in Lebanon in the post-Taif era. Such ties provide significant financial support (about $23 million per month),[67] which allows the party to dispense public services, such as building schools and hospitals, to a wider cross-section of the Shiite community. Such economic power and the political astuteness of its leadership—particularly its spiritual leader, Hussain Fadllah—transformed the party into one of the main Shiite political groups in Lebanon. The Taif regime reinforces the development of sectopolitics à la the Party of God.

The wars between and within the sects led to the "retribalization" of the Lebanese communal and spatial identities. This is not atypical even in cultures aversive to propinquity: Traumatized groups are inclined to reconnect with family, home, and community for shelter and security.[68] Social conflicts in pluralistic societies are very complex, and consequently political parties have great difficulty in coping and adjusting to social structure changes. The Kataib was transformed gradually from a political party (in the classical Western sense) to a sectarian tribe. In other words, the social contradictions and political structures in a multiconfessional society like Lebanon succeeded in reinventing political modes of representation more consistent with traditional characteristics and with the nature of political representation.[69] This same observation applies to the PSP and other political groups.

SYRIA'S REALIGNMENTS AND THE CONSOLIDATION OF SECTOPOLITICS

During the post-1982 phase, Lebanon's sectarian political parties succeeded in overshadowing secular political parties due to the new political conditions created by the 1982 Israeli invasion and Syria's new foreign policy and alliances. Syria adjusted its policies to accommodate the new balance of forces created by Israel's invasion of Lebanon, which produced two major and interrelated changes: the military withdrawal of the PLO, the LNM's main political ally, and the military and political setbacks suffered by the leftist political parties.

Syria's choices were illustrated by its new alliances with sect representatives rather than with the leftist political parties, as was the case before the 1982 Israeli invasion.[70] Such political realignment contributed to the reinforcement of sectopolitical parties at the expense of the secular democratic forces. As a consequence, the Lebanese Communist Party, the Organization of Communist Work, the Syrian Social National Party, and the Popular Democratic Party, among others, became ineffective in Lebanon's body politics. The Taif Accord, therefore, came to reflect the new regional realignment reinforced after the 1991 Gulf War whence Syria sided with Saudi Arabia and the Western alliance against Iraq. Under such new conditions the Lebanese left and its reform secular program became out of tune with the realities created by the Gulf War. Of course, in this context the collapse of the Soviet Union is crucial to our understanding of the international conditions that have helped redraw the political map of the Middle East and of Syria's realignments in the region.

Despite the equal power sharing between Muslims and Christians, which eliminated one important source of conflict, the Taif Accord fell short in opening the political process by secularizing political representation. In essence, the contestation of political power continues to be defined by sectarian divides; therefore, secular parties still confront the same social and political sectarian structures that have shaped the political landscape since independence. In addition, fifteen years of warfare has left open wounds and scars between sects that make secular parties' task of building national organizations more formidable. The healing process is difficult when there are constant reminders of the past, in this case, a system that is based on sectarian divides and sectopolitics.

It is doubtful whether the new consociational arrangement will have better prospects than the 1943 National Pact, now that the alignment between class and sect hegemony has been broken by the Muslim elite gaining more political power. Like any political compromise, the Taif Accord is subject to criticism and attacks. The Maronite elite, which lost part of its political power and status, already resents the manner in which the accord has been implemented and voices its grievances about its underrepresentation in the political system. Ironically, the Maronite elite is using the same arguments that its Muslim counterpart used throughout most part of the postindependence phase.[71] Furthermore, Sunni and Shiite segments of the political elite increasingly compete for political power, which brings a new phase in power struggle and sectopolitical polarization. The Sunni-Shiite power struggle also is bringing to light the constitutional loopholes (if not crisis) of Taif, where the three branches of government enjoy veto power. Thus the political process is left vulnerable with no effective institutional mechanisms when a dispute arises between government branches.[72] This fact explains why, in every crisis situation, Syria has to mediate among the three branches of Lebanon's government to settle political differences.

Under such conditions, political parties are most likely to be shaped by the new modes of power organization and power contestation generated by the Taif regime. Between 1949 and 1996, the PSP was transformed from a secular party into a sectarian one not only in its main social base of support but also in its political ideology and behavior. The sectarian social structure and the sectarian system of political representation both have constrained the PSP's abilities to develop as a secular party. Furthermore, these same structures and system inhibited the development of other secular political parties.

The sectarian regimes of 1943 and of 1989 have placed secular political parties at a disadvantage (in fact, penalized them) vis-à-vis other political groups (sectarian political bosses, church/mosque leaders, and sectopolitical parties). Secular political parties have to contest power (ideologically and politically) with representatives of all these groups combined (i.e., objectively), because they seek popular support among all sects.[73] Yet the political system appreciates sect representation and offers no opportunity for other forms of political representation. Second, the system of sectarian political representation adds another obstacle to the ascendance of secular parties to power. It limits their ability to select/nominate their best candidates to run for public office due to sectarian quotas and the electoral system. These parties also must compromise by dealing with traditional family networks, sect representatives, nepotism, clientelism, and other ills generated by the political system.[74]

Finally, the political system of sectarian representation has generated fertile grounds for sectopolitical orientations by appealing to and reinforcing society's most primordial archaic values. This in turn has affected intersect dynamics and intrasect relations.

As for social and economic reforms, the Taif regime again fell short. Thus far no measures have been designed or formulated to bridge intersect socioeconomic disparities, and no national development plan exists for the different regions of Lebanon, particularly the most underdeveloped areas. The current government of Rafik Harriri seems concerned principally with reconstructing Beirut, which is arousing dismay in the peripheral regions.[75] His focus is, in effect, maintaining the regional and henceforth, sectarian disparities (due to the overlap between the two). Thus the old social structure will be perpetuated without significant change, despite the political change. The Muslim, and particularly the Shiite, community continues to be the most underprivileged group in Lebanon, notwithstanding significant gains in political power by its elite. These few examples demonstrate some problems of the Taif Accord and some of the obstacles that are confronting Lebanon's pacification, secularization, and democratization.

If the structure of power and its sectopolitical system are limiting the development of national parties that cross-cut sectarian lines, what are the prospects of secular party politics in Lebanon?

The Lebanese political system has reinforced sectarian loyalties at the expense of rational national values and democratic norms. This condition wrecked political party efforts to act as integrative devices in the body politics of Lebanon. Sectopolitics, in its social, political, ideological, and institutional manifestations, remains the main obstacle confronting secular party politics in Lebanon.

Notwithstanding the case of the PSP, this study's findings acquire additional importance if placed within the context of the overall weakness of secular parties in Lebanon. The most plausible explanation for this weakness is that the structure of domination and the sectarian political system in Lebanon offered strong resistance to any form of political organization that attempted to overcome sect lines and barriers. Or as Kenneth Waltz put it, power structures encourage certain behaviors and penalize those who do not respond to the encouragement.[76] The PSP responded to the sectarian encouragement and the party was rewarded by increasing its Druze partisans, which reinforced its position in the arrangement of power. The other secular forces, such the LCP and SSNP, which resisted, were penalized and consequently marginalized in the political process.

In this context, therefore, democracy and political parties are not solely an exercise in political or social engineering decided by "above"; rather, they are an interlocked composite of a complex historical process subject to the influence of the elite as well as the forces of social structures and the type of political institutions and power arrangements in place. The dialectics between political actors and their sociopolitical environment are constantly changing. At times, elites appear to enjoy a wider margin of freedom to make political choices and decisions; and at other times social contradictions overwhelm them and limit these choices considerably.

In Lebanon, exogenous factors have further complicated the operationalization of these dialectics. The dialectics between these elements, particularly the endogenous factors, will determine in the last instance the course of political development (i.e., political outcomes), its modes, patterns, and political institutions. Hence, in the cases of PSP, LCP, and SSNP I found ingredients of structural "determinism," individual "voluntarism," and contingencies. The core issue is how actors can manipulate their environment, and to what extent the environment limits and shapes their scope of action and choices.

One basic question poses itself here: How to remedy/or recompense for the defects of political parties in a society like Lebanon? Is democracy at best a doomed aspiration? Chapter 7 offers some reflections and insights that could help in answering these questions.

CHAPTER SEVEN

Crossroads between Sectocracy and Democracy: The Future of Political Parties

DURING THE PAST TWO DECADES, there has been a resurgence of attention on the role of political parties in the transition to democratic rule and democratic consolidation. The dominant theme in this growing body of literature is the autonomy of politics in respect to social structure and class. Dunkwart Rustow's seminal article (1970) was groundbreaking in this respect; he argued that "democracy is acquired by a process of conscious decision at least on the part of the top political leadership . . . a small circle of leaders is likely to play a disproportionate role."[1] In the same vein, although more cautious, Samuel Huntington contended "that democratic regimes that last have seldom, if ever, been instituted by mass popular action. Almost always, democracy has come as much from the top as from the bottom."[2]

Among recent works that have highlighted socioeconomic factors that make democracy possible are those of Terry Lynn Karl,[3] who argued that political choices made by elites do not depend solely on elite goals and commitment to democracy. However, choices and alternatives available to elites are largely influenced by socioeconomic and political structures that provide them with both incentives and constraints for political action. Dietrich Ruechsmeyer, Evelyne Stephens, and John Stephens also adopted a structural analysis according to which democracy is a by-product of the convergence of domestic and international factors that produce a balance of power favorable to democratic rule at home. In this scheme, the choices of political elites are largely a product of the correlation of forces between social classes domestically and international conditions.[4] When the coincidence of domestic power relations (class) and international conditions is favorable to democratic development, political elites are compelled to seek democratic means to manage their conflicts.

Where does this research fit in the current debate? My findings support the thesis that political parties are influenced by social structures and institutional arrangements. Political outcomes, such as regime breakdowns, are a by-product of the dynamic relationship between agency and structure. This research shows that political structures (in this case the system of domination that institutionalizes a sectarian hierarchy of power between the Muslim and Christian Maronite communities) largely formed the axis along which the political struggle between social groups took place between 1943 and 1989. Accordingly, political parties and political bosses competed in a zero-sum struggle for political and economic resources.

My findings, based on information provided by PSP and other leaders who were involved in the decision-making process at critical junctures in Lebanon's consociational democracy, demonstrate the impact of social and political structure on the political choices available to the PSP's leadership. Sectarian social and political structures constrained the abilities of the PSP to expand its power base beyond the Muslim community (mainly Druze), despite its leaders' commitment (particularly under Kamal Jumblatt) to establish a national political organization.

The dynamic relationship between structure and political behavior is not unilinear or obvious but is constantly mediated by various factors (such as a leader's ideology, social class, sect, goals, ambitions, and perceptions), which help in shaping political choices and outcomes. Furthermore, the interplay of international and regional elements with domestic political processes has influenced the dynamics between structures and political behavior. In the case of the PSP, the party's opposition since its inception to the rules of the game (structure of power and its corollary institutions) has largely shaped its political behavior. This behavior has been underpinned by socioeconomic (e.g., increasing in levels of poverty, growth in regional/sectarian disparities, rates of unemployment) and political changes (such as the Cold War, Arab nationalism, the rise of the PLO) that prompted the party to pursue actions that it believed would advance its political objectives.

Finally, the PSP as a part of a network of interacting political actors locked in a chicken game of mutual intransigence (noncooperation) put in motion a dynamic that induced the regime's instability.[5] The PSP's abilities to compromise were limited in 1958 and 1975 due to its predispositions (informed by power structures and institutional arrangement) and to the choices that its leaders made in response to environmental stimuli and contingencies.

At another level, the perils of Lebanon's consociational democracy offer an example of the political and social consequences of status inequity between sects. The unequal distribution of political power between Muslims and Christians in a system based on sectarian representation provided fertile ground for political conflict and civil strife for most of country's modern history. The unequal status distribution was compounded with class inequalities, wherein the Christian community enjoyed more economic resources than the Muslim community at large. As demonstrated in this study, this class/sect alignment has polarized the polity and reduced the abilities of elites to compromise. My study supports Lipset's and Rokkan's observation that in order to limit conflict during the processes of democratization, it is important to equalize the status of different religious denominations; their observation was based on their study of Western democracies that were able to defuse successfully sectarian conflicts early on in their effort to democratize.

The current burgeoning of ethnic and religious wars make it imperative that we understand the grammar of conflict in multiethnic or multisectarian societies. If the argument presented in the previous chapters is valid, then the stability of democratic rules, the success of democratic transitions, and the establishment of healthy political parties in heterogeneous societies will depend on satisfying the following five conditions:

1. A just distribution of political power between groups through meritocracy and secular values;
2. The establishment of political rules acceptable to a significant

portion of the elite and endorsed by the populace (e.g., through plebiscites);

3. Institutionalized mechanisms to mediate and arbitrate conflicts acceptable by the elite;
4. A broad social base of political participation incorporating mechanisms and institutions for the representation of key social groups (such as labor unions, peasant organizations, women groups, environmental and human rights organizations, and minorities representatives);
5. The avoidance of the growth of extreme inequalities between social classes, regions, or ethnic groups, and the avoidance of any alignments characterized by class and ethnic (sect, cultural, racial, or regional) domination.

If these conditions are satisfied, then the polity can defend itself against exogenous destabilizing factors, either in the form of direct foreign intervention or through the processes of globalization and the free movement of capital and labor, or both. Both exogenous factors become important only when social groups are unable to form a political game acceptable to the key players in the polity. In that instance, as the case of the PSP informs us, sects seek alliances with foreign forces in an effort to change the balance of forces in order to establish new rules that are more in their favor.[6]

This research demonstrates that the PSP leadership during the 1958 and 1975 crises was motivated primarily by denying its political opponents the chance to enhance their power rather than by finding avenues to settle the disputes peacefully.[7] PSP leaders did not accept the rules of the political game, which, in their view, reinforced an unjust social and political order. The "rules of the game," in my opinion, constitutes the core problem in Lebanon. In this connection it is important to draw on the work of Giovanni Sartori, who noted the significance of interelite consensus in democratizing societies. Sartori broke down the notion of consensus into three possible meanings: the "ultimate values" of democracy; the "rules of the political game, or procedures"; and the specific "governmental policies." He noted that elites' commitment to the ultimate values of democracy is a facilitator but not an indispensable condition for the existence of a democracy, whereas the elites' acceptance of the "rules of the political game" is indeed a fundamental prerequisite for democratization. He added that discussion and descensus in the third sense are part of the essence of democratic governance.[8]

This case study of the PSP lends support to Sartori's contention that the rules of the political game are essential for maintaining political stability. The PSP leadership, its allies in the LNM, and the majority of the Muslim elite believed that the rules of the political game perpetuated a political order that discriminated against them because it denied them an equal access to power and state resources. Thus the rules were not accepted because they were perceived as unfair and producing disadvantageous outcomes in terms of distribution and allocation of government resources, licensing for imports/exports, public service appointments, and foreign policy orientations. This fact explains why disputes over government policies degenerated into violent confrontations and were not solved in accordance with democratic rules and procedures. It is safe to say that the Palestinian factor (i.e., one of the most important exogenous elements in the 1975 crisis) would not have been as destabilizing if the Muslim elite and the leftist parties had accepted the rules of the political game.

The question that emerges here is whether the Taif Accord establishes rules that enhance the stability of the political system and ease the transition to democratic rule.

THE TAIF REGIME AND THE NEW RULES OF THE POLITICAL GAME

The Taif Accord reduced the constitutional power of the Maronite president and enhanced the power of both the Sunni prime minister and the Shiite house speaker. A troika was established wherein the Maronite, the Sunni, and the Shiite enjoy equal power in decision making, designing government policies, and making political appointments, and have equal quotas of public employees. The other sects in Lebanon, such as the Druze and non-Maronite Christians, are junior partners in the new sectarian system. In structural terms, Taif rearranged the distribution of political power and modified the mode of interaction among the sects, but it certainly did not change the ordering principle of the system, which remains sectarian political representation.

In fact, the Taif Accord reinforced the sectarian system of political representation by stipulating in the constitution the distribution of office according to sects, whereas the previous constitution did not do so. The unwritten National Pact of 1943 was a "gentlemen's agreement" that devised a norm for the sectarian distribution of public offices that the political class observed for about three decades. Thus one of the immediate outcomes of the Taif regime is the perpetuation of an environment that can hardly improve sociopolitical conditions for the development of secular national organizations. It may be argued that the accord laid the foundation for a sectocracy and overlooked the basic groundwork needed to build a democracy.

Sectopolitics will remain the main avenue for the contestation of power, unless the political class applies a provision of Taif that calls for the formation of a high-ranking committee of the president, the prime minister, and the speaker of the parliament to lay down plans to eradicate the sectarian system of political representation. However, there are no signs that the sectarian political bosses will implement that provision any time soon. In effect, the new regime creates a sense of déjà vu, because Article 95 of the previous constitution also stipulated that sectarian representation was only a temporary measure to guarantee a "just" distribution of power among sects. Until sectarian political representation is abolished, the Taif regime will continue to heighten sectopolitical polarization, just as the previous regime did. This is particularly true if the new regime produces a new structure of power whereby Muslims exercise political hegemony over the political process—that is, if one system of domination is supplanted by another.

In a sectarian society like Lebanon, it is impossible to satisfy all sects all the time. Such a system is in a constant state of turbulence due to the structure of power contestation, particularly so because the processes of socioeconomic development are by their very nature destabilizing. For example, dislocations of social groups (as an outcome of economic development) can easily strain a sectarian system when the consensus of political elite over the rules of the political game are absent and/or shaky. Sect representatives, as the case of Lebanon indicates, have to respond to their constituency to alleviate some of their hardships by presenting the sect's demands to the government. Such a move could trigger a countermove by another sect. Thus instead of addressing the problem as a national concern that requires a concerted and programmatic effort, sect representatives engage in a zero-sum struggle over finite resources. The sectarian system compels sects and their representatives to engage in a struggle for resources that keeps the polity polarized and the political process in a state of turmoil. This turmoil stems also from the system of sectarian representation and, as ex-prime minister Salim el-Hoss noted, is based on a balance that is apt to be upset by any demographic change that might take place over time.[9] It also is apt to be upset by capitalist economic development.

Therefore, as long as Lebanon's political system depends on sects' representation and its elite refuses to secularize the system,[10] open the political process, and establish meritocracy, Taif or any similar sectarian arrangement will perpetuate the polity's sectopolitical polarization. Given the long history of sectopolitical strife that has been compounded by feelings of mutual distrust between the Maronite and Muslim communities, the Taif Accord does not seem to nurture the development of interelite consensus. The lack of an interelite consensus underscored by intersect social inequalities makes the future of democracy in Lebanon at best precarious. Consequently, its polity will continue to be vulnerable and prone to the fluctuations and changes in the global and regional environments.

Finally, the seven years of the Taif Accord's enforcement have displayed an asymmetry of bargaining power in favor of the Sunni elite at the expense of those of other sects. What made this possible is Rafik al Hariri's strong ties with international finance capital, plus the political support he has received also at the regional and international level.

This condition illustrates the precariousness of what Caroline Hartzell and Donald Rothchild called "conflict management systems based on asymmetrical pacted settlements."[11] The Taif Accord exhibited two major shortcomings: The pact was introduced under a balance of power favoring the Muslim elite, due mainly to the international sanctioning of Syria's role in Lebanon after 1989, which was reinforced during and after the 1991 Gulf War; and the distorted application of the pact, which heightened the asymmetries of power distribution and led major sects, such as the Maronites, and junior ones, such as the Druze, to complain. The prospects for its survival after Syria, guarantor and enforcer, withdraws from Lebanon are dim.

ARE SOCIAL AND CIVIC ORGANIZATIONS AN ALTERNATIVE?

The failures of political parties in Lebanon raise a series of critical questions: Is democracy possible without viable secular political parties? How could a democracy be reconciled with the sectocracy of Taif? Do the crises of political parties in Lebanon correspond in part to larger world's trends?

In the late 1980s and early 1990s, new political groups were formed that, in my opinion, represent the birth of a new pulse in the civil society.[12] Tens of social organizations with diverse agendas were founded, ranging from the environment, human rights, women issues, to youth organizations. These groups predominantly cross-cut sectarian lines in terms of membership and/or issues, they reflect the interests of segments of the civil society that were long overshadowed by civil war. These groups have the potential of evolving into grass-roots movements with democratic practices, values, and goals, elements that are critical for the future foundation of democratic politics in a highly fragmented polity.

Grass-roots organizations could circumvent the negative effects of sectopolitics on their behavior and membership, which secular political parties failed to do. Parties are mainly concerned with channeling and expressing their own interests, and their raison d'être is to contest power. In such cases sectopolitics (as the main mode of power contestation) takes a heavier toll on political parties than on groups that are not competing for or contesting political power.

These social organizations are more concerned with seemingly microissues that certainly have far-reaching political and social effects. For example, a number of women's organizations are active in several areas and issues, one of which is to introduce legislation to improve women's legal standing in the workplace and in the law. Lebanese law discriminates against women and subjects women to second-class citizens. Thus women's struggle to change these laws requires an increasing popular awareness to the importance of democratizing gender relations, and also to its positive effects on the social and political democratization processes.

Furthermore, the emergence of environmentalist and human rights groups bring national attention to these two important areas. Citizens now hear about the impact of environmental degradation on their livelihood, water resources, and land; more important, these concerns create a rallying point that unifies a good cross-section of the Lebanese people. Some human rights organizations focus on the importance of observing due process, prisoners' rights, and political freedoms.

Another organization that acquired special status due to its distinct role during the years of the bloody conflict, when it opposed the civil war and its patrons, is the General Confederation of Workers Trade Unions, the largest labor union in Lebanon. Since the mid-1980s, the General Union has been instrumental in organizing antiwar demonstrations, against the wishes of the warring factions, which added to its credibility as an independent social force. The Union's antiwar activities culminated in the famous 1987 demonstration, which attracted about 100,000 Christians and Muslims to march jointly to protest the civil war and militia practices.[13] During that demonstration people started to dismantle the barricades that divided Beirut into Christian and Muslim sectors.[14] The union survived the sectarian fragmentation that crippled most secular parties. Since 1990 it has struggled to safeguard political freedoms, workers' rights, and social democracy, making it in effect one of the most important political forces in the country. It became the rallying point for most secular forces, individuals, and groups.[15] However, the union's 1997 election suffered a severe blow when it split into two factions, both claiming legitimacy. It seems that the state is determined to co-opt the labor movement and to weaken its mobilizing capacities against neoliberal economic policies.

The activities of all these social organizations can be considered the beginning of a new political reality. These groups' activism is attracting national attention and support, which helps reinforce secular democratic values in the civil society. In this sense, the birth of democracy in Lebanon is part of a historical process whose building blocks are being laid down at this very moment. The failures of Lebanon's consociational democracy and particularly its political parties' inability to fulfill their role as instruments to channel and express aggregate (secular) interests may have provided favorable conditions for the emergence of this new wave of social organizations.

Interestingly enough, the emergence of social movements, both structured and unstructured, in Lebanon coincides with a worldwide trend in which traditional political parties are losing their relevance in the democratic process. Electoral results in the 1990s have demonstrated considerable support for new social movements and nontraditional political parties in Germany, Austria, Italy, and France.[16] In Peru the current president, Alberto Fujimori, was a university dean; Antanas Mockus, the ex-mayor of Bogota and now a presidential candidate, and the mayors of three other major cities in Colombia are from civic movements. Irene Saez, Miss Universe in 1981 and a political independent, is currently a leading presidential candidate in Venezuela, once the showcase of Latin American institutionalized party-systems. Many similar cases are available.

Similarly, in Lebanon a number of intellectuals are building or participating in social movements with loose organizational structures rather than in political parties. Samir Franjieh, a well-known leftist intellectual and nephew of late ex-president Sleiman Franjieh, is now leading one such movement; others like him with liberal/secular ideological inclinations are moving in the same direction. This new tendency reveals that some intellectuals are reconsidering the principle of mass party and the issues of power and democracy in light of their own personal experiences and the experiences of labor and socialist parties in Europe and the Soviet Union, and the current crisis of political parties in Western democracies. What is at stake in this discourse is the fate of political parties as "the" instruments of social change and democratization.

Are "social movements" the political wave of the future and the vehicles of popular voice rather than political parties? Perhaps yes. It can be plausibly argued that the complexities of the globalization of the world economy, and neoliberal anti–state-welfare economic policies, have reduced the capacity of mass political parties to use the state as an instrument for allocating resources to benefit their constituencies,[17] thus reducing their importance in developed industrial societies. Such conditions (globalization and neoliberal economic policies) acquires more importance in sharply divided societies, where political parties are in essence weak and the state is poor. Thus social movements, spontaneous and structured, are becoming essential vehicles to address and solve pressing social needs, and allocate and distribute resources (through nongovernmental organizations and international aid). As a consequence of these activities, social movements are forging a new social fabric based on grass-roots democracy where people assume a more active role in the social and political organization of their lives and gradually participate in the dismantling of archaic and sectarian barriers.

Even as I wrote this conclusion, Walid Jumblatt, PSP leader and a member of the Hariri cabinet, offered yet another proof for my argument. He said in an interview conducted by *Al Hayat* newspaper in February 1995 that "Lebanon's political parties are finished, including the PSP, they do not possess the vision to answer for the growing complexities of [Lebanon's] social problems."[18] Jumblatt proposed instead the creation of a "green party" that can lead the campaign against corruption, sectarian feudal lords, and the business elite and unite all Lebanese."[19] These views underscore the deep crisis in Lebanon's political parties and its "sectocratic" system, and offer further proofs for the need for alternative forms of political and social organizations.

What is also relevant to my core argument is Jumblatt's contention that, in the absence of secularism and "genuine national cohesion" and given that the Taif Accord redivided political power among the three largest sects with their regional and international linkages (the Sunni with the Arab Sunni, the Shiite with Iran, and the Maronites with the Vatican and the Christian world), the small sects (such as the Druze) have been left alone, and thus have no alternative but to defend themselves.[20] Along with representatives of other key sects, Jumblatt operates in a "self-help" Waltzian system, which is conducive neither to democratization nor to the construction of "real" political parties. Their view owes as much to sectopolitics as to the new sectarian power arrangements, or sectocracy.

As long as Lebanon's political representation is based on sects—as units of representation—political competition will polarize these sects, undermining the possibility of creating national cohesion chiefly because sectarian power structures reinforce vertical social divisions, making democracy very precarious. And political parties aspiring to transcend and overcome sectopolitics have little hope, if any, within the parameters of such an arrangement. Hence, in Lebanon, the parties of sects will remain the major form of political representation until the polity is secularized.

CONCLUDING THOUGHTS

Democracy in Third World multiethnic and sectarian societies is still a scarce commodity. Often violence is the main mode to contest political power or to compete for resources. Political parties, the main channels of political representation, become entangled in ethnopolitics, reinforcing the vertical social divisions and curtailing the development of rational democratic values.

Lebanon has valuable lessons to offer in this regard, one of which is the role the power structure plays in determining the choices available to political leaders, particularly in times of crisis. The PSP and other political parties assumed radical stands during such times, which contributed to civil strife.

However, most leaders of Lebanon's political parties have changed significantly and now are committed to the democratic process as the sole mechanism to negotiate social and political conflicts.[21] Lebanon's political leaders have drawn important lessons from the 1975 to 1989 experience, one of which is that in severely divided societies, political compromise is the key to democratic rule and stability. However, it remains to be seen how this political learning is put into practice in times of political distress.

NOTES

CHAPTER ONE
POLITICAL PARTIES IN SECTARIAN SOCIETIES

1. See Donald Horowitz, *Ethnic Groups in Conflict* (Berkeley: University of California Press, 1985), pp. 334-340. Let me mention the cases of the Guyanese People's Progressive Party, for example, a Marxist group that viewed the subordinate condition of the Indian population in British Guyana as a progressive social force and thus came to represent ethnic interests rather than secular ones. Sri Lanka presents another interesting case where leftist parties compromised their universal secular ideologies in ethnically divided societies. The Communists and Trotskites accepted the Sinhalese position in the struggle for language parity between the Tamil and the Sinhala. Another example is the Malay Communist Party; it became the main representative of the Chinese community, which, despite its economic prosperity, was suppressed culturally and politically by the Malay dominant group. The Communist Party saw the Chinese subordinate position as a progressive element and a linchpin for political change. The Communist Party of India in the Punjab was largely a Sikh party. Horowitz argues that the party was composed of prosperous Sikh peasants of the Jat caste and accordingly supported the Sikh demand for a separate state within India. In Peru and Guatemala, the guerilla movements were largely based on the indigenous Indian population, the most suppressed group in the power structure in both societies. These cases reflect a pattern where political parties, particularly of the left, build their constituencies on the dominant social cleavage. Accordingly, their programs reflect that cleavage and the political means to resolve it.
2. I borrowed the term "contestation of political power" from Robert Dahl, *Polyarchy, Political Participation and Opposition* (New Haven, CT: Yale University Press, 1971).
3. As quoted in Robert A. Alford, "Class Voting in the Anglo-American Political Systems," in Seymour Lipset and Stein Rokkan (Eds.), *Party Systems and Voter Alignments: Cross National Perspectives* (New York: The Free Press, 1967), p. 69.
4. See Kay Lawson, "When Linkage Fails," in Kay Lawson and Peter Merkl (Eds.), *When Parties Fail: Emerging Alternative Organizations* (Princeton, NJ: Princeton University Press, 1988), pp. 13-38.

5. C. B. Macpherson, "Social Conflict, Political Parties and Democracy," in William Crotty, Donald Freeman, and Douglas S. Gatlin (Eds.), *Political Parties and Political Behavior* (Boston: Allyn and Bacon, 1966), p. 58.
6. Scott Mainwaring, "Political Parties and Democratization in Brazil and the Southern Cone," *Comparative Politics* 21, no. 1 (October 1988), p. 113.
7. For a discussion of the strategic calculations involved in an individual actor's decision making, see Anthony Downs, *An Economic Theory of Democracy* (New York: Harper & Row, 1957), p. 42.
8. See Terry Lynn Karl, "Dilemmas of Democratization in Latin America," *Comparative Politics* 23 no. 1 (October 1990), p. 7.
9. James Buchanan and Gordon Tullock, *The Calculus of Consent* (Ann Arbor: University of Michigan Press, 1960), p. 20.
10. I conducted all the interviews reading the questions from my notebook. The questions were divided into two sections. The first section seeks the member's class, sect, educational background, and the causes behind his decision to join the party. The second section is open-ended and deals with the member's experience during the periods that are of interest for this research. Each interview lasted around an hour and half; some were a little longer, particularly with more talkative members. I was impressed by the candidness of the most of those interviewed; however, some have asked to remain anonymous. I held follow-up interviews with some members whom I thought were important to my research due to the position they occupied during specific periods.
11. The interviews conducted with informants and officials of other political parties were more informal and sought data and information for cross-references, validation, and comparative purposes. This research also relies on the PSP files and records, which provide information about the members, including profession, area and date of birth, and date of joining the party. I classified more than 17,800 members according to sect and social class.
12. Wilham Chambers, *Parties in a New Nation* (New York: Oxford University Press, 1963), p. 80.
13. M. Weiner and J. LaPalombra, "Impact of Parties on Political Development," in Joseph LaPalombra and Myron Weiner (Eds.), *Political Parties and Political Development* (Princeton, NJ: Princeton University Press, 1966), p. 414.
14. Ibid.
15. See Arend Lijphart, *Democracy in Plural Societies: A Comparative Exploration* (New Haven, CT: Yale University Press, 1977), chap. 2.
16. Seymour Lipset and Stein Rokkan, *Party System and Voter Alignments: Cross National Perspectives* (New York: The Free Press), pp. 4-5.
17. Robert Alford, "Class Voting in Anglo-American Political Systems," in Lipset and Rokkan, op. cit., p. 69.
18. Horowitz, op. cit., p. 291.
19. The term ethnopolitics is borrowed from Joseph Rothschild, *Ethnopolitics, A Conceptual Framework* (New York: Columbia University Press, 1981).
20. Horowitz, op. cit., pp. 99-105.
21. Ibid., p. 105.

22. See Kamal Jumblatt, *Robou Qarn min al Nidal* (A Quarter Century of Struggle) (Beirut: Dar al Takadomieh, 1975); see also his books *Fi Majarah al Siyassah al Lubananiyah* (On Lebanese Politics) (Moukhtara: Dar al Takadumieh, 1987) and *I Speak For Lebanon* (London: Zed Press, 1982).
23. Horowitz, op. cit., p. 683.
24. Charles Bergquist, Ricardo Penaranda, and Gonzalo Sanchez,(Eds.) *Violence in Colombia* (Wilmington, DE: Scholarly Resources, 1992). See particularly Luis Alberto Restrepo, "The Crisis of the Current Political Regime and Its Possible Outcomes," pp. 273-292.
25. Horowitz, op. cit., p. 683.
26. See particularly Robert Melson and Howard Wolpe, "Modernization and the Politics of Communalism: A Theoretical Perspective," *American Political Science Review* 64 (December 1970), pp. 1112-1130; see also Thomas Hodgkin, *African Political Parties* (Middlesex: Penguin Books, 1961); Daniel Lerner, *The Passing of Traditional Societies in the Middle East.* (New York: The Free Press, 1964).
27. See Roger Brown, *Social Psychology* (New York: New York Press, 1965) as quoted in Linton Freeman, "Social Network and the Structure Experiment" in Linton Freeman, Douglas White, and A. Kimball Rommey (Eds.), *Research Methods in Social Network Analysis* (Arlington, VA: George Mason University Press, 1989), p. 14.
28. This definition of political structure has been influenced by Kenneth Waltz's conception of structure in which he argues that "structure is not a collection of political institutions but rather the arrangement of them. The constitution of a state describes some parts of the arrangement." See Kenneth Waltz, *Theory of International Politics* (Berkeley: University of California Press, 1979), p. 80.

CHAPTER TWO
THE POLITICAL ECONOMY OF SECTOPOLITICS

1. Random House *Webster's College Dictionary* (New York: Random House, 1991).
2. In one interview, Sana Abu Shakra, the Lebanese Communist Party's political bureau member and party's spokesman, contends that the multiconfessional composition of the Lebanese polity and the sectarian political system have limited the party's abilities to extend its power base within the non-Muslim community, particularly among the Maronites. Abu Shakra believed that all secular parties in Lebanon confronted this dilemma. He added that sectopolitics have influenced the confessional composition of the party in which the Shiite members constitute more the 40 percent of its 7,000 members. Sana Abu Shakra, interview with author, Beirut, June 3, 1994.
3. Richard van Leeuwen, "Monastic Estates and Agricultural Transformation in Mount Lebanon in the 18th Century," *International Journal of Middle East Studies* 23 (1991), p. 606.

4. Ibid., p. 601. See also Iliya Harik, *Politics and Change in a Traditional Society: 1711-1845* (Princeton, NJ: Princeton University Press, 1968), p. 112; D. Chavallier, *La Societe de Mont Liban a L'epoque de la Revolution industrielle en Europe* (Paris, na. 1971).
5. For a more detailed account about the role of the Maronite church in the nineteenth-century capitalist transformation, see Harik, op. cit., especially chap. 9; see also Masoud Daher, *Al Juzur al Tarikhiya lil Masaalt Al Taifiya al Lubananiya 1697-1861* (The Historical Roots of the Lebanese Sectarian Question) (Beirut: Maahad al-Inma al-Arabi, 1981).
6. Daher, op. cit.
7. See Malcom Kerr, *Lebanon in the Last Years of Feudalism 1849-1868, A Contemporary Account by Antoun Dahir al Aqiqi and Other Documents* (Beirut: American University of Beirut, 1959); see also Masoud Daher, *Al Intifidat al Lubnaniya Dud Nizam al Makataji* (The Lebanese Revolts Against the Mukataji Feudal System) (Beirut: Dar al Farabi, 1988). Daher focuses on the peasant revolts against the feudal taxation system that had made their living conditions intolerable.
8. Kamal Salibi, *The Modern History of Lebanon* (New York: Praeger,1965), p.106.
9. Abdo Baaklini, *Legislative and Political Development: Lebanon 1842-1972* (Chapel Hill, NC: Duke University Press, 1976), p. 45.
10. Ibid., p. 48.
11. Michael Hudson, *The Precarious Republic: Modernization in Lebanon* (Boulder, CO: Westview Press, 1985), p. 44.
12. Dietrich Rueschmeyer, Evelyne Stephens, and John Stephens, *Capitalist Development and Democracy* (Chicago: University of Chicago Press, 1992), p. 48.
13. Max Weber, *From Max Weber: Essays in Sociology,* H. H. Gerth & C. Wright Mills (ed. and trans.) (New York: Oxford University Press, 1946), p. 194.
14. Ibid., pp. 186-187.
15. Ibid., p. 189.
16. Michael Johnson, *Class and Client in Beirut; The Sunni Muslim Community and the Lebanese State 1840-1985* (London: Ithaca Press, 1986), especially chap. 5. Johnson discusses how the presidency, in the absence of a strong legislature, facilitated the business of the dominant economic class, particularly its Christian component.
17. Baaklini, op. cit., p. 220.
18. 18.Jonson, op. cit., chap. 5.
19. Salim Nasr and Claude Dubar, *Al Tabakat Al-Ijtimaiya fi Lubnan* (Social Classes in Lebanon) (Beirut: Moussasat al-Abhath al-Arabiya, 1982), pp. 98-100.
20. See Boutros Labaki, "L'Economie politique du Liban independant, 1943-1975," in Nadim Shahadi and Dana Mills (Eds.), *Lebanon: History of Conflict and Consensus* (London: Center for Lebanese Studies, 1988), p. 175.
21. Joseph Chamie, "The Lebanese Civil War: An Investigation into the Causes" *World Affairs* 139, no. 3 (Winter 1976-1977), pp. 178-180.

22. Kamal Hamdan, "Malameh Altajawulat fi al-Tarkiba al-Taifiya lil-Iktisad al-Lubnani fi al-Tisinat" (Glimpses Over the Tranformations of Sectarian Composition f Lebanese Economy in the 1990s) *An-Nahar,* January 12 1998, p. 13.
23. Kamal Salibi, *House of Many Mansions: The History of Lebanon Revisited* (Berkeley: University of California Press, 1988), chaps. 11 and 12.
24. Chamie, op. cit., p. 181.
25. Charles Hauss and David Rayside, "The Development of New Parties in Western Democracies Since 1945," in Louis Maisel and Joseph Cooper (Eds.), *Political Parties: Development and Decay* (Beverly Hills, CA: Sage Publications, 1978), p. 39.
26. Ibid., p. 39.
27. See Peter Drucker, *Post-Capitalist Society* (New York: Harper Collins, 1993), pp. 44-45.
28. Hudson, op. cit.
29. Arend Lijphart, *Democracy in Plural Societies* (New Haven, CT: Yale University Press, 1977). Lijphart makes the case that the Maronite elite's unwillingness to cede some of its power to the Muslims after it lost its numerical superiority contributed to the collapse of the consociational democracy in 1975. Dekmejian makes a similar argument, in which he blames the Maronite elite's refusal to adjust the distribution of political power to satisfy Muslim demands as causing the disruption of harmony. See R. H. Dekmejian, "Consocioational Democracy in Crisis: The Case of Lebanon," *Comparative Politics* 10, no. 2 (1978), pp. 251-266. For an evaluation of the consociational theory and its applicability on the Lebanese case, see Michael Hudson, "The Problem of Authoritative Power in Lebanese Politics: Why Consciatioalism Failed," in Shahada and Mills, op. cit., pp. 224-239.
30. See George Jada', "The Role of Sectarian Consciousness in the Ideology and Organization of the Lebanese Left, 1975-1976," Master's thesis, American University of Beirut, 1985.
31. Abu Shakra, interview. Abu Shakra made it clear that the party sided with the Muslims in their quest for an equitable share of power. He revealed that such a political stand had created tension within party ranks when a faction emerged calling for a review of this policy, but the party remained committed to its alliance with the Muslim elite. He explained that the structure of power in Lebanon and the distribution of political forces left the party limited political choices and alternatives, particularly when the struggle in Lebanon became intrinsically enmeshed with the regional and international struggle between the East and West.
32. For a study on how the Lebanese left became embroiled in its slogans and programs in sectopolitics (i.e., adopting the Muslim elite demand to expand its political representation), see Jada', op. cit.
33. Rogis Dib, former secretary-general of the Kataib Party and former member of the leadership of the Lebanese Forces, interview with author, Beirut, March 1994. Dib explained that the Kataib and the Lebanese Forces are political parties that were established to represent and defend the interests of the

Christians in Lebanon. He added that both forces have had no intention or plans to expand their political base beyond the Christian community.

34. See Yusuf Kazma, *Al-Taifiya fi Lubnan min Khilal Munakashat Majlis al-Nuwab* (Sectarianism in Lebanon Through the Discussions in the Parliament) (Beirut: Dar al-Hamra, 1989), pp. 50-53.
35. 34.Hudson, op. cit., p. 93.
36. Ibid.

CHAPTER THREE CHARACTERISTICS OF PSP LEADERSHIP, ITS COMPOSITION AND POLITICAL BEHAVIOR

1. See Juan Linz, *The Breakdown of Democratic Regimes: Crisis, Breakdown, and Reequilibriation* (Baltimore: Johns Hopkins University Press, 1978).
2. See Arturo Valenzuela, *The Breakdown of Democratic Regimes: Chile* (Baltimore: Johns Hopkins University Press, 1987).
3. Ibid., p. 22.
4. See Samuel Popkin, *The Rational Peasant* (Berkeley: University of California Press, 1979); see also James Denardo, *Power in Numbers* (Princeton, NJ: Princeton University Press, 1985); and Forrest Colburn, *Post Revolutionary Nicaragua* (Berkeley: University of California Press, 1986). These authors use rational choice arguments to explain political behavior. Popkin treats the question of why peasants who are assumed to maximize their own welfare by not rebelling decide sometimes to join revolutionary movements. Denardo raises the question of why members of radical organizations who can plausibly be assumed to maximize their chance of reaching power without militancy choose a particular political alternative that diminishes their personal chances. Finally, Colburn uses the rational choice model to explain economic decisions in post-revolutionary Nicaragua that could be explained not in structural but in institutional terms. But perhaps one of the most interesting works is by George Tsebelis, *Nested Games: Rational Choice in Comparative Politics* (Berkeley: University of California Press, 1990). Tsebelis addresses the central question of why actors under certain circumstances choose an alternative that appears to be against their own interests; he feels it is because actors could be involved in multiple arenas or what he terms nested games. Of special interest is his chapter 6, where he adopts a rational choice to consociationalism. My analysis is influenced by Tsebelis's treatment of the institutional structures (rules of the game) that influence the actors' political behavior.
5. Khalil Ahmad Khalil, *Thaurat al Amir al-Hadith* (Revolution of the Modern Prince) (Beirut: Dar al-Maktoubat al Sharkiya, 1987), p. 68.
6. Ibid., p. 103.
7. Abdallah al-Aleily, a founding member of the PSP, interview with author, Beirut, July 1987.
8. Ibid.
9. Ibid.

10. Abdallah al-Aleily, interview with author, Beirut, Summer 1989. Sheikh al-Aleily expressed that Sit Nazira called him for a meeting to voice her objections to the idea of founding a socialist party and asked him if he could convince Kamal to give up the idea. Al-Aleily responded "that if she cares about Kamal leadership, the PSP is the proper modern vehicle through which he could emerge as a national leader."
11. According to al-Aleily, George Hanna espoused Marxist thought. Ibid.
12. Fareed Jubran became a member of the leadership council in the 1950s and was also member of Lebanese parliament. Interview with author, Beirut, Summer 1989.
13. See Max Weber, *From Max Weber: Essays in Sociology,* H. H. Gerth and C. Wright Mills (eds. and trans.), (New York: Oxford University Press, 1946). Weber maintains that individuals join political parties motivated by class/and or status interests.
14. Arend Lijphart referred to Lebanon as a consociational democracy that is built on an engineered political arrangement between the elites of Christians and Muslims. See his work *Democracy in Plural Societies* (New Haven, CT: Yale University Press, 1977), pp. 147-150.
15. Al-Aleily, interview.
16. Ibid.
17. Fouad Salman, leadership council member, interview with author, Beirut, March 1994.
18. Shaker Shaiban, interview with author, Beirut, Summer 1989.
19. Ibid.
20. Ibid.
21. 1994 Salman interview.
22. Clovis Maksoud, interview with author, Washington, D.C., September, 1989.
23. The PSP organizational hierarchy is composed of members of the leadership council, advising members, and working members. The leadership council is elected from the advising members and the rank-and-file representatives. In this research the changes in the advising members composition are discussed when deemed necessary.
24. Clovis Maksoud, interview with author, Washington, D.C., Summer, 1990.
25. Ibid.
26. Ibid.
27. Sleiman Basha, interview with author, Beirut, Summer 1989. At the time of the interview, Basha was second-in-command of the PSP department of labor.
28. Ibid.
29. The 1958 crisis lasted about seven months during which time military clashes took place between forces loyal to President Chamoun and opposition forces in most of major Lebanese cities. Several hundred were killed and injured during the hostilities. The PSP controlled a significant part of the Shouf after seizing control of police stations in the area. The crisis ended after American military intervention.
30. According to Fouad Salman (interview 1994), Talhouk left the party because he felt that the PSP did not endorse his candidacy for parliament.

31. Ibid.
32. Ibid.
33. Fouad Salman, member of the PSP polite bureau, interview with author, Beirut, Summer 1988.
34. M. S. Aganwi, *The Lebanese Crisis, 1958: A Documentary Study* (Bombay: Asia Publishing House, 1965), p. 2.
35. Ibid.
36. See Maalumat, *"al Hizb al Shiyoui Saboun Aman fi al Siyasah al Lubnaniya"* (The Lebanese Communist Party Seventy Years in Lebanese and Arab Politics) *Assafir* (Beirut: Lebanon, 1993). In the Communist Party conference held in 1993, the number of Maronite delegates, which largely reflected their relative size in the party rank-and-file cadre, was 10 percent of the total number of delegates, whereas the Shiite amounted 41 percent of delegates, 19 percent were Sunni, 9 percent were Druze, and 17 percent were Christian Orthodox. In the case of Syrian National Party see Bishara Doumani "The Syrian Social Nationalist Party: An Analysis of its Social Base" (Master thesis, American University of Beirut, 1983). Again the Maronite appear the less represented in the SSNP leadership. (See chapter 6). See also Michael Suleiman, *Political Parties in Lebanon* (Ithaca, NY: Cornell University Press, 1967), p. 101. This suggests a pattern that the members of the dominant status group were less attracted to leftist political groups than the other (subordinate) social groups.
37. Kamal Jumblatt, *Robou Qarn Min al Nidal* (A Quarter Century of Struggle) (Beirut: Dar al Takadomieh 1975), p. 26.
38. Frank Parkin, *Marxism and Class Theory: A Bourgeois Critique* (New York: Columbia University Press, 1979), pp. 90-97.
39. See chapter 2 where evidence is provided about the superior status of Christians in terms of the distribution of income, higher-paid skilled jobs, and other indicators. In addition, the Maronite elite played a dominant position within the state apparatus.
40. Jumblatt, op. cit.
41. Shaiban interview.
42. Jumblatt, op. cit., p. 48.
43. Shaiban interview.
44. Shaiban interview.
45. Jubran interview.
46. 1994 Salman interview.
47. Almost all of the fourteen party officials that were interviewed expressed this opinion.
48. Adam Przeworski, *Democracy and the Market, Political and Economic Reforms in Eastern Europe and Latin America* (New York: Cambridge University Press, 1991), p. 19.
49. See *Le Liban: Face a son Developpement 1960-1961* (Beirut: Institut International de Reccherces et de Formations en veu du developpment Harmonise [IRFED], 1963). The commission's report underscored the gravity of the problem of income inequality between the different social classes.

The report also pointed out the imbalanced developments between the areas where the Muslim regions were the most neglected by the government.

50. 1989 Salman interview. Salman's opinion was shared by Naim Ghanam, Fareed Jubran, Joseph Kazi, Shaker Shaiban, and other PSP members of the Leadership Council.
51. 1989 Salman interview.
52. Jumblatt, op. cit., pp. 64-65.
53. In the 1960s the leftist movement flourished in Lebanon in the wake of the growing crisis at home, coupled with the growth of anti-West movement in the Arab world. In the late 1960s an increasing number of new left movements were established, such as the Arab Work Socialist Party, the Communist Work Organization, and the Trostkite movement. The Communist Party also witnessed also a growth in its membership during this period. Nazeeh Hamzeh, secretary general of the Democratic Popular Party, interview with author, Beirut, March 1994.
54. In the early 1970s, unemployment rates reached about 15 percent of the work force without taking into account the disguised unemployment. See Salim Nasr and Claude Dubar, *Al-Tabakat al-Ijtimaiyah fi Lubnan* (Social Classes in Lebanon) (Beirut: al Moussasat al-Abhath al-Arabiya, 1982).
55. IRFED, op. cit.
56. See Jumblatt, op. cit. See also his book *I Speak for Lebanon* (London: Zed Press, 1982).
57. Most of the PSP officials I interviewed shared this view.
58. Khalil Ahmad Khalil, interview with author, Beirut, Summer 1989. Khalil was in the leadership council between 1969 and 1975 period. He was reelected to the 1994 leadership council.
59. See Samuel Huntington, *Political Order in Changing Societies* (New Haven, CT: Yale University Press, 1968), chaps. 1 and 2.
60. See Lijphart, *Democracy in Plural Societies*, op. cit., pp. 149-150. Lijphart rightly pointed to the main dilemma of Lebanon's power-sharing system: the inflexible institutionalization of consociational principles. He explains that the segmental allocation of the highest offices and the preset electoral proportionality, both which favored the Christian sects that constituted a majority in the 1932 census, could not allow a smooth adjustment to the gradual Christian loss of majority status to the Muslims.
61. Kareem Pakradouni, interview with author, Beirut, April 1996. Pakradouni was then the leader of the liberal faction within the Kataib Party.
62. Rogis Dib, ex-secretary general of the Kataib Party, interview with author, Beirut, April 1994.
63. Muhsin Ibrahim, secretary-general of the Organization of Communist Work and executive general secretary of the Lebanese National Movement (1974-1982), argued that the Tripartite alliance was an attempt by the Maronite elite to regain political dominance after its 1958 setback. According to Ibrahim, the 1967 Arab defeat encouraged the Maronite elite to benefit from the new regional balance of forces. Interview with author, Beirut, April 1996.

64. Valenzuela, op. cit., p. xii.
65. Muhsin Ibrahim, op. cit., p. 42. He makes the point that after the April 1969 confrontations between the Palestinian Resistance (leftist) and the Lebanese army (rightist) militias, Jumblatt played a moderating role in his capacity as minister of the interior in an effort to find a modus vivendi between the conflicting forces. In fact, Jumblatt did not even support the April 13 demonstration that sparked the bloody confrontations that spread to several main cities such as Beirut, Tripoli, Sidon, and Tyre, until after the fact. Ibrahim also argues that Jumblatt's mediating efforts continued after hostilities began, again, in April 1975.
66. See *Al-Birnamaj al-Marhali lilislah* (The Interim Reform Program) (Beirut: Manshurat al Haraka al Wataniya al Lubnaniya, 1974).
67. Sana Abu Shakra, interview with author, Beirut, June 1994. This view was shared by a number of officials of the PSP and other Communist Party cadres that I interviewed in the summers of 1987 and 1988.
68. See Muhsin Ibrahim, *Al Harb Wa Tajrabat al-Haraka al-Wataniya* (The War and the Experience of the National Movement) (Beirut: Beirut al Masa', 1983), pp. 26-33. Muhsin explains in his book that the National Movement, even after the April 13 events, was still committed to a peaceful democratic struggle to achieve its goals specified in the reform program.
69. Abu Shakra interview.
70. Fuad Shbaklou, independent member of the National Movement Central Council (1975-1982), and a close associate of Jumblatt, interview with author, Beirut, Summer 1989.
71. See Ibrahim, op. cit.
72. As quoted in Khalil, op. cit., p. 582.
73. The concept of critical mass is borrowed from Antonio Gramsci. See *Selections from Prison Notebooks* (New York: International Publishers, 1971), pp. 165-173.
74. This is based on interviews with PSP officials and discussions with Fouad Salman, Shaker Shaiban, and Naim Ghanam. All either were or are currently serving as members of the PSP leadership council. Shaiban served in the 1975 council; thereafter he retired and remained a loyal supporter of the PSP until his death.
75. Khalil, op. cit., pp. 527, 538.
76. Shaiban interview. Shaiban, a member of the PSP leadership council, revealed that he was against the policy of isolating the Kataib due to its negative sectarian effects. According to Shaiban, Jumblatt nonetheless insisted on pursuing such a policy.
77. Abu Shakra interview. Abu Shakra revealed that the Communist Party, as well as the PSP, underestimated the appeal of sectopolitics among a wide cross-section of Christians, particularly the Maronites. This underestimation led to miscalculations in their policies and strategies.
78. See Jumblatt, *I Speak for Lebanon*, op. cit., pp. 80-81.
79. Ibid., pp. 40-63.
80. See George Tsebelis, op. cit., pp. 161-163.

81. See Arend Lijphart, *The Politics of Accommodation: Pluralism and Democracy in the Netherlands* (Berkeley: University of California Press, 1968); see also Lijphart, *Democracy in Plural Societies,* op. cit.; V.R. Lorwin, "Belgium: Religion, Class, Language in National Politics." in R. A. Dahl (Ed.), *Political Opposition in Western Democracies* (New Haven, CT: Yale University Press, 1966); K. McRae, *Consociational Democracy: Political Accommodation in Segmented Societies* (Toronto: McClelland and Stewart, 1974).
82. For a discussion of the applicability of the consociational model on the political arrangements in Lebanon since independence, see Michael Hudson, "The Problem of Authoritative Power in Lebanese Politics: Why Consociationalism Failed," in Nadim Shehadi and Dana Mills (Eds.), *Lebanon: A History of Conflict and Consensus* (London: Center of Lebanese Studies, 1988), pp. 224-39. See also R. J. Dekmejian, "Consociational Democracy in Crisis: The Case of Lebanon," *Comparative Politics* 10, no. 2 (1978), pp. 251-266.
83. The National Movement remained ineffective until 1983, when Walid Jumblatt officially ended the alliance.
84. See Nazih Richani, "Walid Jumblatt," in Bernard Reich (Ed.), *Contemporary Leaders of the Middle East* (Boulder, CO: Greenwood Press, 1990).
85. 1989 Jubran interview. Jubran was the vice president of the party, the logical successor when President Kamal Jumblatt was gunned down. Taufic Barakat, advisor member of the PSP, interview with author, Summer 1989. Barakat also highlighted the debate that took place within the PSP leadership about the succession.
86. 1989 Jubran interview.
87. The Maronites established independence from feudal lords in the eighteenth century; see chapter 2.
88. Shareef Fayad, secretary-general of the PSP, interview with author, Beirut, March 1994. Fayad revealed that the number of advising members have increased from 60 in 1977 to 327 in 1994. He attributed that increase to PSP needs during the war but believed that growth was unhealthy to party development, particularly because a great number of the current advisors are not qualified for the position. Most were militia leaders with little or no political education and experience. Fayad also indicated that one of the first undertakings of the newly elected leadership would be the suspension of the advising position in an attempt to reinvigorate the party apparatus.

CHAPTER FOUR
THE SYSTEM OF DOMINATION AND THE PSP RANK AND FILE, CLASS AND SECTARIAN COMPOSITION, 1949-1994

1. Joseph Kazi, member of the PSP leadership council since the late 1970s, interview with author, Dair al Kamar, Lebanon, Summer 1989.
2. Kamal Jumblatt, *Robou Qarn min al-Nidal* (A Quarter Century of Struggle) (Beirut: Dar al-Takadumiah, 1975), p. 25.

3. Muhsin Daloul, an ex-member of the leadership council during the 1970s and 1980s, interview with author, Beirut, Summer, 1989.
4. Ibid.
5. Ibid.
6. Ibid.
7. Ibid.
8. Ibid.
9. Abdallah al-Aleily, establishing member of the PSP and member of its leadership council in the 1950s, interview with author, Beirut, Summer 1989.
10. Ibid.
11. Sleiman al-Basha, a member of the leadership of the Workers Liberation Front (a PSP workers' union), interview with author, Beirut, Summer 1989.
12. Ibid.
13. Michael Hudson, *The Precarious Republic* (Boulder, CO: Westview Press, 1984), pp.155-157.
14. Ibid.
15. Ibid.
16. Ibid.
17. Ibid.
18. Ibid.
19. See Raymond Delpart, "Liban L'evolution du Niveau de Vie Milieu Rural 1960-1970," (Beyrouth: Ministere du Plan, Doc. Roneote, 1970), p. 9.
20. PSP records.
21. The term menu people is borrowed from Michael Johnson, *Class and Client in Beirut: The Sunni Muslim Community and the Lebanese State* (London: Ithaca Press, 1986). Menu people is a floating social group that rely on multiple sources of income, self-employed in the formal and/or informal economy.
22. Fouad Salman, a member of the leadership council since 1975, interview with author, Beirut, Summer 1986.
23. Naim Ghanam, a member of the leadership council since the 1970s, interview with author, al-Shouf, Lebanon, Summer 1988. See also Jumblatt, *Robou Qarn*, op. cit. pp. 188-189.
24. Sana Abu Shakra, interview with author, Beirut, June 1994. See also Michael Suleiman, *Political Parties in Lebanon* (Ithaca, NY: Cornell University Press, 1967).
25. Abu Shakra interview. See also Kamal Salibi, *House of Many Mansions: The History of Lebanon Revisited* (Berkeley, CA: University of California Press, 1988), chaps. 10 and 11.
26. See Michael Johnson, *Class and Client in Beirut*, op. cit.
27. Ibid.
28. Ibid.
29. Ibid.

30. 1986 Salman interview.
31. Salim Nasr and Claude Dubar, *Al Tabakat al-Ijtimaiya fi Lubnan* (Social Classes in Lebanon) (Beirut: Moussasat al-abhath al Arabiya, 1982), pp. 108-121.
32. Daloul interview.
33. See Nabeel Khalifa, *Al Shia fi Lubnan* (The Shiites in Lebanon) (Beirut: Biblos Press, 1984). See also Boutros Labaki, "L'Economie Politique du Liban independant 1943-1975," in Nadim Shehadi and Dana Mills (Eds.), *Lebanon: a History of Conflict and Consensus* (London: Center for Lebanese Studies, 1988), pp. 177-179.
34. Joseph Kazi interview.
35. Ibid.
36. Nasr and Dubar, op. cit., p. 79.
37. Johnson, op. cit.
38. Ibid.
39. Ibid.
40. Fouad Shbaklou, an independent leftist, was a member of the central committee of the Lebanese National Movement and close associate of Jumblatt, interview with author, Beirut, Summer 1987.
41. PSP records.
42. Daloul interview. This view was also shared by PSP officials Shaker Shaiban, Anwar Fateiry, and Fouad Salman.
43. Anwar Fateiry was a member of the leadership council in the 1980s and a PSP student leader in the 1970s, interview with author, al-Shouf, 1987.
44. Nasr and Dubar, op. cit., p. 92.
45. Khalil Ahmad Khalil, leadership council member in the 1970s and 1980s, interview with author, Beirut, Summer 1986.
46. See Nicos Poulantzas, *Classes in Contemporary Capitalism* (London: Verso, 1975).
47. Khalil interview.
48. Ibid.
49. Ibid.
50. Ibid.
51. Khalil was in charge of the "school of cadre"; interview.
52. Fareed Jubran, member of the leadership council since the 1950s and party vice president, interview with author, Beirut, Summer 1987.
53. See John Entelis, *Pluralism and Party Transformation in Lebanon: Al-Kataib Party, 1936-1970* (Leiden: E. J. Brill, 1974), pp. 119-121.
54. These estimates are based on data provided by Sharif Fayad, the secretary general of the PSP. Interview with author, Beirut, March 1994.
55. "Adwa' ala al-Jimiyat-al-Omumiya al-Arbein lil-Hizb al-Ishtinaki wa Wathikatuno al-Siyasiyah" (Lights on the PSP's Fortieth General Assembly and Its Politcal Platform), *Al-Nahal* 23 (January 1998), p. 10.

CHAPTER FIVE
THE PSP DURING THE YEARS OF TURMOIL AND RECONCILIATION, 1979–1996

1. Janeen Rubeiz served as a PSP advising member and was in charge of the party's foreign relations in the early 1980s; interview with author, Beirut, Summer 1987.
2. Some PSP officials who have requested anonymity allege that the Syrian intelligence services were behind the killing of Kamal Jumblatt in 1977.
3. Fouad Salman, interview with author, Beirut, February 1994.
4. See Joseph Abu Khalil, *Kusat al Mawarinah fi al* Harb (The Story of the Maronites in the War) (Beirut: Sharikat al Matbouat liltaozei wal Nasher, 1990), pp. 41-55, 179-208.
5. See Zeev Shiff, *Israel's Lebanon War* (New York: Simon and Schuster, 1984). Schiff presents an interesting account of the relationship of the Lebanese Maronite militia with Israel and what they sought from this alliance.
6. Salman interview.
7. For an elaborate analysis on "war systems" see Nazih Richani, "The Political Economy of Violence: The War-System in Colombia" *Journal of Interamerican Studies and World Affairs* 39, no. 2, (Summer 1997), pp. 37-81.
8. This is based on my own observations during my research in Lebanon. In the last few years, grass-roots organizations have emerged in a number of villages, trying to open their own channels of communication and coordination with other groups independent from the traditional Druze leadership. In two cases, these groups openly challenged the hierarchy of power by refusing to accept conditions set by Jumblatt and Arislan.
9. This is based on an informal discussion with a Druze political aspirant who is running for municipal election.
10. See Kenneth Waltz, *The Theory of International Politics,* (Berkeley: University of California Press, 1979), chap. 6.

CHAPTER SIX
THE PREDICAMENT OF LEBANON'S POLITICAL PARTIES

1. "Al Hizb al Shiyoui al-Lubnani, Saboun Aman" (The Lebanese Communist Party, Seventy Years), *Maalumat* (September 1993) (Beirut: al Markaz al Arabi Lilmaalumat), p. 79.
2. Ibid. These figures were issued by the Lebanese Communist Party.
3. Ghasan Rifai, member of the LCP political bureau, interview with author, Beirut, April 1996.
4. Ibid.
5. The Lebanese Communist Party formed part of the Syrian Communist Party until the early 1960s, when it broke away and became an independent political party.

6. Kareem Mroueh, polit bureau member of the LCP, interview with author, Beirut, April 1996.
7. Muhsin Ibrahim, secretary-general of the Communist Work Organization and executive general secretary of Lebanese National Movement (1974-1983), interview with author, Beirut, April 1996.
8. The position of assistant secretary-general was designed to accommodate Hawi's faction. Hawi became secretary general in 1977.
9. This observation is based on a number of sources. Sana Abu Shakra, spokesperson of the LCP, interview with author, Beirut 1994; and see also Al Hizb al Shiyoui al Lubanani, op. cit., p.49. The LCP started military training in 1969, where fifty members were being trained. Ghasan Rifai, polit bureau member of the LCP, interview with author, Beirut, April 1996.
10. See Kenneth Waltz, *The Theory of International Politics,* (Berkeley: University of California Press, 1979), p. 108.
11. George Hawi, *""Yatazakar""* (Memories), *Al Wasat* no. 231 (1-7 July 1996), p. 34.
12. Rifai interview.
13. Hawi, op. cit., p. 43.
14. This is a reference to an ambush carried out by rightist militias with possible links with security and intelligence organizations (regional and international), against a bus carrying unarmed Palestinians that were en route to a refugee camp in east Beirut. This incident is considered the trigger of the war.
15. 15.George Hawi, *"Yatazakar"* (Memories) *Al Wasat,* no. 228 (10-16 June 1996), p. 32.
16. Ibid., pp. 32-33.
17. Sana Abu Shakra, interview with author, Beirut, June 3, 1994.
18. Ibid.
19. Ibid.
20. Ibid. This point came across in an informal talk with Samir Saad, a member of the Central Committee of the LCP, Beirut, Summer 1993.
21. These observations are based on my interviews with Sana Abu Shakra and informal talks with Samir Saad.
22. Abu Shakra interview.
23. See *Wathaek wa Takareer al Sadera an al Moutamar al Watani Al Sades* (Documents and Reports of the Sixth National Conference) (Beirut: LCP Publications, 1992), p. 97. George Hawi contends that the LCP had 15,000 members during the 1983's Mountain War. See George Hawi, *"Yatazakar"* (Memories) *Al Wasat,* no.231 (1-7 July 1996), p. 36.
24. This figure was provided to author by LCP spokesperson Abu Shakra.
25. Kareem Mroueh, *"Mahawer Arabiya lil-Jadal wal Nidal fi Marhalat al-Intiqal bain Haqabatain"* (Arab Sides for Dialectics and Struggle in a Period of Transition between two Phases), *Al-Tarik,* no. 5 (September 1996), p. 16.
26. See Kamal Salibi, *A House of Many Mansions: The History of Lebanon Revisited* (Berkeley: University of California Press, 1988), pp. 134-135.
27. See Bishara Doumani, "The Syrian National Party: An Analysis of its Social Base" Master's thesis, American University of Beirut, 1983.

28. Data obtained from Murwan Fares, interview with author, Beirut, April 1996. Fares is a member of the SSNP Majles Ala (highest Commission), which is the leading organ of the party; he belongs to the al-Tawaré faction.
29. See Michael Hudson, *The Precarious Republic* (Boulder, CO: Westview Press, 1985), pp. 172-173.
30. Inam Raed, president of the SSNP, interview with author, Beirut, April 1996. Raed leads a faction of the SSNP; he assumed the leadership of the party during the civil war. The SSNP is divided into two main factions.
31. Ibid.
32. Fares interview. Fares belongs to the faction opposing Raed.
33. See *Wathaek al Haraka al Wataniah al Wataniah* (Documents of the Lebanese National Movement) (Beirut: LNM Publications, 1981), p. 12.
34. Abu Shakra interview.
35. See Donald Horowitz, *Ethnic Groups in Conflict* (Berkeley: University of California Press, 1985) pp. 291-364.
36. In a meeting organized by the Arab anti-Discrimination Committee (ADC), Mr. Walid Jumblatt expressed the view that his party and its allies have little influence over the course of events in Lebanon although they are actively engaged in those events. Interview with author, Washington D.C., Fall 1989.
37. See Samir Khalaf, *Lebanon's Predicament* (New York: Columbia University Press, 1987), pp. 118-120.
38. Nazih Richani, "The Druze of Mount Lebanon: Class Formation in a Civil War" *Middle East Report*, no. 162 (January-February 1990).
39. These figures were reported by the American Task Force for Lebanon, *Conference on Lebanon Working Paper* (Washington D.C.: ATFL Publications, 1991), p. 24.
40. These estimates were obtained from Kareem Pakradouni, political bureau member of the Kataib Party, interview with author, Beirut, April 1996.
41. See Khalaf, op. cit., pp. 102-120.
42. Ibid., pp. 104-109.
43. Richard Hans Laursen, "The Kataib: A Comprehensive Study of a Lebanese Party," Master's thesis, American University of Beirut, 1951.
44. Kareem Pakradouni interview.
45. Ibid.
46. Ibid.
47. Ibid.
48. Muhsin Ibrahim interview.
49. Ibrahim revealed that the only one who wanted to compromise was Kamal Jumblatt, but Jumblatt's political line was overtaken by the war programs of the extreme left, led by Ibrahim, and the extreme right, led by the Kataib. Interview with author.
50. Ibrahim interview.
51. Rogis Dib, secretary-general of the Kataib (1989-1992), interview with author, Beirut, March 9, 1994.
52. For an account of the ascendance of the Lebanese Forces, see Hazem Saghieh, *Taareeb al Kataib al Lubananiya* (The Arabization of the Lebanese Kataib)

(Beirut: Dar Al Jadeed, 1991), pp.131-257. See also Lewis Snider, "The Lebanese Forces: Wartime Origins and Political Significance," Paper presented at a meeting of the California seminar on international security and foreign policy, November 8, 1983.

53. Albert Hourani as quoted in Saghieh, op. cit., p. 171.
54. John Entelis, *Pluralism and Party Transformation in Lebanon, Al Kataib, 1936-1970* (Leiden: E. J. Brill, 1974), p. 114.
55. Saghieh, op. cit., pp. 172-173, 201-205.
56. These data were compiled from two sources: Rogis Dib interview and Entelis, op. cit., p. 113.
57. Rogis Dib interview. See also Nazih Richani, "Center-Periphery Relations: The Dialectics of Social Change, the Case of Lebanon 1975-1991." Paper presented at the Middle East Studies Association annual convention. Washington, D.C., November 23-26, 1991.
58. Entelis, op. cit., p. 121. Robert Farah, LF Spokesperson, interview with author, Washington, D.C., summer, 1991.
59. About the crisis of the Kataib, see *Al Hayatt*, January 16, 1993.
60. Dib interview.
61. Nadeem Ltaif, interview with author, Beirut, April 1996.
62. Dib interview; Pakradouni interview.
63. Abu Said al-Khansa, Party of God's Maylis Siyaseh member, interview with author, Beirut, January 1998.
64. Nizar Hamze, "Islamic Parties in Lebanon," Paper presented at the American Political Science Association Convention, San Francisco, 1996.
65. Ibid.
66. Hazem Sagieh, "Ashnat Iyam Fi Lubnan--Lam tattuz Ahaden wa la Hazat Shian" (Ten Days in Lebanon Did Not Shake Nobody and Nothing), *Al Hayat* (February 19, 1998), p. 19.
67. Informant, interview with author, Beirut, April 1996. According to Nizar Hamze's paper, this funding was cut by almost 90 percent after 1990. Hamze, op. cit. The party invested most of the money donated by Iran, which allowed it to become largely self-sufficient.
68. Samir Khalaf, "Culture, Collective Memory and the Restoration of Civility" in Deidre Collings (Ed.), *Peace for Lebanon? From War to Reconstruction* (Boulder, CO: Lynne Reinner Publishers, 1994), p. 283.
69. Samir Khalaf, op. cit.
70. See George Hawi, *"Yatazakar"* (Memories), *Al Wasat*, no. 228 (10-16 June 1996), p. 32. Hawi contends that the correlation of forces between the secular left and sectopolitical parties contributed to the transformation of the struggle in Lebanon into a sectarian strife, particularly after 1984. He alludes to the Syrian role in Lebanon after the Israeli invasion of 1982 in reinforcing sectopolitical polarization.
71. See the speech of Mar Nisralah Sfeir, the Patriarch of the Christian Maronite church in Lebanon, in Al Nahar (Beirut), April 2, 1994. In this speech Sfeir outlined the position that Christian Maronites in Lebanon ask for equitable representation in the government. Sfeir is believed to represent the political

position of the Maronite elite, particularly since no strong Maronite leader commands enough support to lead the community. Perhaps the strongest political figures within the Maronite community are General Oun and Reymond Edde; however, both live in exile due to their strong opposition to the Syrian presence in Lebanon.

72. For example, lately Sunni Prime Minister Rafik Hariri decided to suspend (not resign) his duties as prime minister because he wanted to exert pressure on Shiite speaker of the parliament Nabih Berri, to accept the reshuffling of the current government. Berri wants certain portfolios in the reshuffle, which Hariri refused to concede. This example not only demonstrates the lack of consensus but also that the government lacks mechanisms to resolve a crisis of this magnitude.
73. In areas dominated by sectopolitical groups (Amal, Kataib, PSP, Party of God, Lebanese Forces), the activities of opposing groups were banned. The ban included the activities of secular parties, which suffered murder and constant terror at the hands of some of these political groups.
74. Such a view was expressed by all PSP officials that I interviewed for this research. It also was shared by a number of Lebanese Communist Party officials and informants (cadre) who argued that Lebanon's sectarian electoral system, which is based on districts, has limited the ability of the secular parties to compete successfully in national elections. The district system reinforces the power of sect bosses within their own localities through the traditional channels of power, such as clientelism, favors, nepotism, notable networks, status, and family connections.
75. For a detailed discussion about Lebanon's reconstruction plans see Hassan Sharif, "Regional Development and Integration," in Collings, op. cit., p. 161.
76. Kenneth Waltz, op. cit., p.106.

CHAPTER SEVEN
CROSSROADS BETWEEN SECTOCRACY AND DEMOCRACY: THE FUTURE OF POLITICAL PARTIES

1. As quoted in Scott Mainwaring, "Transitions to Democracy," in Scott Mainwaring, Guillermo O'Donnell, and J. Samuel Valenzuela (Eds.), *Issues in Democratic Consolidation: The New South American Democracies in Comparative Perspective* (South Bend, IN: University of Notre Dame Press, 1992), p. 302.
2. Ibid., p. 303.
3. Terry Karl, *Petroleum and Political Pacts: The Transition to Democracy in Venezuela* (Washington, D.C.: The Wilson Center, 1982); see also Karl's article, "Dilemmas of Democratization in Latin America," *Comparative Politics* 23, no. 1 (October 1990), pp. 1-21.
4. See Dietrich Rueschmeyer, Evelyne Stephens, and John Stephens, *Capitalist Development and Democracy* (Chicago: University of Chicago Press, 1992).
5. For a good discussion on the chicken and prisoner's dilemma games, see Michael Taylor, "Cooperation and Rationality: Notes on Collective Action

Problem and Its Solutions," in Karen Schweers Cook and Margaret Levi (Eds.), *The Limits of Rationality* (Chicago: The University of Chicago Press, 1990), pp. 226-233.

6. See *Al-Nahar*, April 13, 1995. In that issue the *Al-Nahar* conducted a panel commemorating the twentieth anniversary of the 1975 civil war. The panelists, who belonged to the different warring parties, confessed that their international and regional ties had influenced their conduct during the civil war and that these ties were used to consolidate their corresponding position.
7. The Lebanese Communist Party also shared this PSP position. LCP spokesman Sana Abu Shakra revealed that his party and the PSP did not accept the rules of the political game; in his opinion, that made it easier for them to abandon democratic practices. This situation was particularly evident in 1958 and 1975, when the PSP and LCP, the two main parties of the leftist National Movement, shifted into armed opposition after they perceived that their demands for political change could not be advanced in the context of democratic institutions and that the regime sought to eliminate them as political forces. Sana Abu Shakra, interview with author, June 1994.
8. As quoted in J. Samuel Valenzuela, *The Breakdown of Democratic Regimes: Chile* (Baltimore, MD: Johns Hopkins University Press, 1987,) p. 82.
9. Salim Al-Hoss, "Prospective Change in Lebanon" in Diedre Collins (Ed.), *Peace for Lebanon? From War to Reconstruction* (Boulder, Co: Lynne Reinner Publishers, 1994), p. 254.
10. For a different opinion on the secularization of the Lebanese polity, see Theodor Hanf, *Coexistence in Wartime Lebanon* (London: Center of Lebanese Studies, 1993). Hanf argues that secularism is not applicable in Lebanon; instead, he advocates the concept of coexistence between sects, similar to the one presented in the National Pact and Taif. Hanf's analysis overlooks one of the main sources of the Lebanese conflict, which is the sectarian system. Established under the pretext of coexistence, the sectarian system institutionalized a structure of power that in fact perpetuated conflict. I suggest secularism not because it is the magic stick that could solve the problems endemic to Lebanon, but because secularism, if enacted, at least could deflate the sectopolitical polarization that has been generated by the sectarian mode of contestation of power.
11. Caroline Hartzell and Donald Rothchild, "Political Pacts as Negotiated Agreements: Comparing Ethnic and Non-ethnic Cases," Paper presented at the 1996 American Political Science Association, Annual Meeting, San Francisco, CA, August 29 - September 1, 1996.
12. In a historical parallel, Guillermo O'Donnell and Philippe Schmitter noted that the transition to democracy in Latin America led to a broad "resurrection of the civil society." Many groups take advantage of the new political circumstances to create or recreate their organizations and articulate their grievances. As quoted in J. Samuel Valenzuela, "Consolidation in Post Transitional Settings," in Mainwaring, O'Donnell, and Valenzuela, (Eds.), op. cit., pp. 84-85.

13. See Conference on Lebanon, *Working Paper* (Washington D.C.: American Task Force for Lebanon, 1991), p. 45.
14. Ibid.
15. Najah Wakeem, deputy in the Lebanese parliament and vocal opposition figure, interview with author, Beirut, March 1994. Wakeem contented that the General Workers Union is a focal point for the secular forces in Lebanon. He revealed that a number of political parties, deputies, and independent are united with the union and are in effect forming a common opposition front. However, in 1997 the state attempted to co-opt the union and this led to a split in the labor movement between a pro-state faction and an opposition.
16. For more details about the emergence of social movements and the decline of political parties, see Kay Lawson and Peter Merkl (Eds.), *When Parties Fail: Emerging Alternative Organizations* (Princeton, NJ: Princeton University Press, 1989); and Enrique Larana, Hank Johnston, and Joseph Gusfield (Eds.), *New Social Movements: From Ideology to Identity* (Philadelphia: Temple University Press, 1994).
17. See Richard Flacks, "The Party's Over," in Larana, Johnston, and Gusfield, op. cit., pp. 335-339.
18. See *Al Hayat*, Sunday, February 12, 1995, p. 6.
19. Ibid.
20. Ibid.
21. Muhsin Ibrahim, interview with author, Beirut, April 1996; Kareem Pakradouni, secretary-general of the Kataib Party, interview with author, Beirut, April 1996; Kareem Mroueh, political bureau member of the Lebanese Communist Party, interview with author, Beirut, March 1996; Ghasan Rifai, political bureau member, Lebanese Communist Party, interview with author, Beirut, March 1996; Inam Raed, the president of a SSNP faction, interview with author, Beirut, March 1996; Murwan Fares, member of Majlis al-Ala (higher commission) of the SSNP (the other main SSNP faction), interview with author, Beirut, April 1996.

Bibliography

Abou Joude, Joseph. *Les Partis Politique au Liban.* Kaslik, Liban: Universite Saint Espirit, 1985.

Abu Ezzedine, Najla. *The Druzes: A New Study of Their History, Faith and Society.* Leiden: E. J. Brill, 1984.

Ajami, Fouad. *The Vanished Imam.* Ithaca, NY: Cornell University Press, 1986.

Alford, A. Robert. "Class Voting in the Anglo American Political Systems." In Seymour Lipset and Stein Rokkan, *Party Systems and Voter Alignments: Cross National Perspectives.* New York: The Free Press, 1967.

Amel, Mahdi. *Fi al-Daula al-Taifiyya* (On the Sectarian State). Beirut: Dar al-Farabi, 1986.

———. *Madkhal ela Nakd al Fikir al Taifi* (An Introduction to the Anti-thesis of Sectarian Thought). Beirut: Dar al Farabi, 1985.

Amin, Samir. *Unequal Development: An Essay on the Social Formations of Peripheral Capitalism.* Brighton: Harvester Press, 1976.

Arlacchi, Pino. *Mafia, Peasants and Great Estates, Society in Traditional Calabria.* New York: Cambridge University Press, 1985.

Aydin, Zulkuf. *Underdevelopment and Rural Structures in Turkey: The Household Economy in Gisgis and Kalhana.* London: Ithaca Press, 1986.

Baloyra, Enrique A., and John D. Martz. *Political Attitudes in Venezuela: Societal Cleavages and Political Opinion.* Austin, TX: Texas University Press, 1979.

Barakat, Halim. *Toward A Viable Lebanon.* Washington, D.C.: Center for Contemporary Arab Studies, Georgetown University, 1988.

Bergquist, Charles, Penaranda Ricardo, and Gonzalo Sanchez (Eds.) *Violence in Colombia.* Wilmington, DE: Scholarly Resources, 1992.

Brown, Roger. *Social Psychology.* New York: New York Press, 1965.

Buchanan, James, and Gordon Tullock. *The Calculus of Consent.* Ann Arbor: University of Michigan Press, 1960.

Calhoun, Craig, Marshall Meyer, and W. Richard Scott. *Structures of Power and Constraint: Papes in Honor of Peter Blau.* New York: Cambridge University Press, 1990.

Cardoso, Henrique, and Enzo Faletto. *Dependency and Development in Latin America.* Berkeley: University of California Press, 1979.

Casanova, Pablo Gonzales. *Democracy in Mexico.* London: Oxford University Press, 1970.

Chambers, W. *Parties in New Nations.* New York: Oxford University Press, 1963.

Chamie, J. "The Lebanese Civil War: An Investigation into the Causes." *World Affairs* 139, no. 3 (Winter 1976/1977) pp. 171-188.

Chilcote, Ronald. *Latin America: The Struggle with Dependency and Beyond.* New York: John Wiley & Sons, 1974.

Chilcote, Ronald H., and Joel Eldestein. *Latin America: Capitalism and Socialist Perspective of Development and Underdevelopment.* Boulder, CO: Westview Press, 1986.

Choueiri, Youssef. *State and Society in Syria and Lebanon.* New York: St. Martin's Press, 1993.

Cobban, Helena. *The Making of Modern Lebanon.* London: Hutchinson, 1985.

Colburn, Forrest. *Post-Revolutionary Nicaragua.* Berkeley: University of California Press, 1986.

Collins, Deidre. *Peace for Lebanon?: From War to Reconstruction.* Boulder, CO: Lynne Reinner, 1994.

Cook, Karen Scheweers, and Margaret Levi (Eds.). *The Limits of Rationality.* Chicago: University of Chicago Press, 1990.

Cutright, J. Willey. "Modernization and Political Representation: 1927-1966." *Studies in Comparative International Development* (1969).

Cutright, Philips. "National Political Development: Measurement and Analysis." *American Sociological Review* 28 (April 1963).

Daher, Masoud. *Al-Juzur al-Tarikhiya Lil-masalat al-Taifiya al-Lubnaniya* (The Historic Origins of the Sectarian Question in Lebanon). Beirut: Arab Development Institute, 1981.

Dahl, Robert. *Polyarchy, Political Participation and Opposition.* New Haven, CT: Yale University Press.

Deeb, Marius. *The Lebanese Civil War.* New York: Praeger, 1980.

Denardo, J. *Power in Numbers.* Princeton, NJ: Princeton University Press, 1985.

Dix, Robert. "Democratization and the Institutionalization of Latin American Political Parties." *Comparative Political Studies* 24, no. 4 (January 1992), pp. 488-511.

Drucker, Peter. *Post Capitalist Society.* New York: Harper Collins, 1993.

Duverger, Maurice. *Political Parties.* London: Methuen and Co., 1954.

Eken, Sena. *Economic Dislocation and Recovery in Lebanon.* Washington, D.C.: International Monetary Fund, 1995.

Eldersveld, J. Samuel. *Political Parties: A Behavioral Analysis.* Chicago: Rand McNally & Company, 1964.

Entelis, John. *Pluralism and Party Transformation in Lebanon: Al-Kataib, 1936-1970.* Leiden: E. J. Brill, 1974.

Flacks, Richard. "The Party's Over." In Enrique Larana et al. (Eds.), *New Social Movements: From Ideology to Identity.* Philadelphia: Temple University Press, 1994.

Frank, Andre Gunder. *Capitalism and Underdevelopment in Latin America: Historical Studies of Chile and Brazil.* New York: Monthly Review Press, 1967.

———. *Latin America: Underdevelopment or Revolution: Essays on the Development of Underdevelopment and the Immediate Enemy.* New York: Monthly Review Press, 1969.

Freeman, Linton, Douglas White, and A. Kimball Rommey (Eds.), *Research Methods in Social Network Analysis.* Arlington, VA: George Mason University Press, 1989.

Geddes, Barbara. "Uses and Limitations of Rational Choice in the Study of Politics in Developing Countries." Paper presented at the American Political Science Association, September 1993.

Gramsci, Antonio. *Prison Notebooks.* New York: International Publisher, 1987.

Green, Donald, and Ian Shapiro. *Pathologies of Rational Choice Theory: A Critique of Applications in Political Science.* New Haven, CT: Yale University Press, 1994.

Halawi, Majed. *A Lebanon Defied: Musa al-Sadr and the Shia Community.* Boulder, CO: Westview Press, 1992.

Hanf, Theodor. *Coexistence in Wartime Lebanon.* London: Center for Lebanese Studies, 1993.

———. "Homo Oeconomicus-Homo Communitaris: Crosscutting Loyalties in a Deeply Divided Society." In Milton Esman and Itamar Rabinovich, (Eds.), *Ethnicity Pluralism and the State in the Middle East.* Ithaca, NY: Cornell University Press, 1988.

Harik, Iliya. *Politics and Change in a Traditional Society: Lebanon, 1711-1845.* Princeton, NJ: Princeton University Press, 1968.

Hass, Michael. "Alternative Paradigms of Ethnic Harmony." Paper presented at the annual meeting of the Political Science Association, September 1993.

Hiro, Dilip. *Lebanon: Fire and Embers: A History of the Lebanese Civil War.* New York: St. Martin's Press, 1993.

Hitti, Philip. *Lebanon in History.* London: Macmillan, 1962.

Hodgkin, Thomas. *African Political Parties.* Middlesex: Penguin Books, 1961.

Horowitz, Donald. *Ethnic Groups in Conflict.* Berkeley: University of California Press, 1985.

Hoss, Salim. "Prospective Change in Lebanon." In Deidre Collins (Ed.), *Peace For Lebanon? From War to Reconstruction.* Boulder, CO: Lynne Reinner Publishers, 1994.

Hourani, Albert. *Minorities in the Arab World.* London: Oxford University Press, 1947.

Hudson, Michael. *The Precarious Republic: Political Modernization in Lebanon.* New York: Random House, 1968; reprint, Boulder, CO: Westview Press, 1985.

———. "The Problem of Authoritative Power in Lebanese Politics: Why Consociationalism Failed." In Nadim Shehadi and Dana Haffar Mills, (Eds.), *Lebanon: A History of Conflict and Consensus.* London: I.B. Tauris and Co., 1988.

Huntington, Samuel. *Political Order in Changing Societies.* New Haven, CT: Yale University Press, 1968.

Ishti, Faris. *Al-Hizb al-Takadumi al-Ishtiraki was Dawruhu fi al- Siyasah al-Lubnaniyah 1949-1975.* (The Progressive Socialist Party and its Role in Lebanese Politics 1949-1975.) al-Muktara, Lebanon: al-Dar al-Taqadumiyah al-Markaz al-Watani lil-Malumat wa al Dirasat, 1989.

Institut de Formation en vue de Developpement. *Le Liban Face a son Developpment.* Beirut: Catholic Press, 1963.

Issawi, Charles. *The Fertile Crescent, 1800-1914: A Documentary Economic History.* New York: Oxford University Press, 1988.

Johnson, Michael. *Class & Client in Beirut: The Sunni Muslim Community and the Lebanese State.* London: Ithaca Press, 1986.

Jones, Bryan D. *Reconceiving Decision-Making in Democratic Politics: Attention, Choice, and Public Policy.* Chicago: The University of Chicago Press, 1994.

Jumblatt, Kamal. *I Speak For Lebanon.* London: Zed Publishers, 1982.

———. *Ma Huwa al-Hizb* (What is the Party). Beirut: The PSP Publications, 1980.

———. *Ada'b al-Hayat* (Codes of Moral Conduct). Beirut: PSP Publications, 1979.

———. *Al-Hizb al-Taqadumi al-Ishtiraki: Robou Karn Min al-Nidal* (The Progressive Socialist Party: A Quarter of Century of Struggle). Beirut: Dar al Taqadumiya, 1975.

Karl, L. Terry. "Dilemmas of Democratization in Latin America." *Comparative Politics* 23, no.1, (October 1990), pp. 1-21.

Kay, Cristobal. *Latin American Theories of Development and Underdevelopment.* London: Routledge, 1989.

Kearney, Robert N., (Ed.). *Politics and Modernization in South and Southeast Asia.* New York: John Wiley and Sons, Inc., 1975.

Kerr, Malcolm. "Political Decision Making in a Confessional Democracy." In Leonard Binder (Ed.), *Politics in Lebanon.* New York: John Wiley and Sons, Inc., 1966.

Khalaf, Samir. *Lebanon's Predicament.* New York: Columbia University Press, 1987.

———. "Primordial Ties and Politics in Lebanon." *Middle Eastern Studies* 4 (April 1968), pp. 243-269.

Khalidi, Walid. *Conflict and Violence in Lebanon: Confrontation in the Middle East.* Cambridge, MA: Center for International Affairs, Harvard University, 1979.

Khalifa, Nabeel. *Al-Shia fi Lubnan* (The Shiites in Lebanon). Beirut: Biblos, 1984.

Khalil, Ahmad Khalil. *Thaurat al-Amir al-Hadith (The Revolution of the Modern Prince).* Beirut: Dar al-Matbouat al-Sharkiya, 1987.

La Palombara, Joseph, and Myron Weiner (Eds.). *Political Parties and Development.* Princeton, NJ: Princeton University Press, 1966.

Laqueur, Walter. *Communism and Nationalism in the Middle East.* New York: Frederick A. Praeger, 1957.

Lawson, Kay, and Peter Merkl (Eds.). *When Parties Fail: Emerging Alternative Organizations.* Princeton, NJ: Princeton University Press, 1989.

Leeuwen, Richard Van. *Notables and Clergy in Mount Lebanon: The Khazins Sheikhs and the Maronite Church 1736-1840.* Leiden: E. J. Brill, 1994.

Lerner, Daniel. The Passing of Traditional Societies in the Middle East. New York: The Free Press, 1964.

Lijphart, A. *Democracy in Plural Societies: A Comparative Exploration.* New Haven, CT: Yale University Press, 1977.

Linz, Juan. *The Breakdown of Democratic Regimes: Crisis, Breakdown and Reequilibration.* Baltimore, MD: Johns Hopkins University Press, 1978.

Lukàcs, George. *History and Class Consciousness.* Cambridge, MA: The MIT Press, 1985.

Maaloumat. "*al Hizb al-Shiyuoi al-Lunani, Saboun Aman*" (The Lebanese Communist Party, Seventy Years). Beirut: al Markaz al Arabi lil Maalumat, 1993.

Macpherson, C. B. "Social Conflict, Political Parties and Democracy." In William Crotty, Donald Freeman, and Douglas Gatlin, (Eds.). *Political Parties and Political Behavior.* Boston: Allyn and Bacon, 1966.

Mafeje, Archie. "The Ideology of Tribalism." *The Journal of Modern African Studies* 9 (February 1971), pp. 253-261.

Mainwaring, Scott. "Transitions to Democracy." In Scott Mainwaring, Guillermo O'Donnell, and J. Samuel Valenzuela (Eds.), *Issues in Democratic Consolidation: The New South American Democracies in Comparative Perspective.* South Bend, IN: University of Notre Dame Press, 1992.

Mainwaring, Scott, and Scully, Timothy. *Building Democratic Institutions: Party Systems in Latin America.* Stanford, CA: Stanford University Press, 1995.

Mansour, Alber. *Al Inkilab ala al-Taif* (Coup Against Taif). Beirut: Dar al-Jadeed, 1993.

McDonald, Ronald H., and J. Mark Ruhl. *Party Politics and Elections in Latin America.* Boulder, CO: Westview Press, 1989.

Meir, Zamir. *The Formation of Modern Lebanon.* London: Croom Helm Press, 1985.

Michell, Robert. *Political Parties.* Glencoe, IL: The Free Press, 1949.

Munk, Ronald. *Politics and Dependency in the Third World: The Case of Latin America.* London: Zed Books, 1984.

Myers, David. "Urban Voting, Structural Cleavage and Party System Evolution: The Case of Venezuela." *Comparative Politics* 8 (October 1975), pp. 133-134.

Nasr, Salim, and Claude Dubar. *Al-Tabakat al-Ijtimaiya fi Lubnan* (Social Classes in Lebanon). Beirut: Moassat al-Abhath al-Arabiya, 1982.

Neumann, Sigmund. *Modern Political Parties.* Chicago: University of Chicago Press, 1956.

Norton, Augustus Richard. *Amal and the Shia, Struggle for the Soul of Lebanon.* Austin, TX: University of Texas Press, 1987.

Phares, Walid. *Lebanese Christian Nationalism: The Rise and Fall of an Ethnic Resistance.* Boulder, CO: Lynne Reinner, 1995.

Popkin, Samuel. *The Rational Peasant.* Berkeley: University of California Press, 1979.

Poulantzas, Nicos. *Classes in Contemporary Capitalism.* London: New Left Books, 1975.

Przeworski, Adam. *Democracy and The Market, Political and Economic Reforms in Eastern Europe and Latin America.* New York: Cambridge University Press, 1991.

Pye, Lucian, and Sydney Verba (Eds.), *Political Culture and Political Development.* Princeton, NJ: Princeton University Press, 1965.

Randall, Vicky, (Ed.). *Political Parties in the Third World.* London: Sage Publications, 1988.

Republic Of Lebanon Ministry of Planning. *Besoins et Possibilites de developpment du Liban.* Beirut: Ministry of Planning, 1960-61.

Richani, Nazih. "Class Formation in a Civil War: The Druze of Mount Lebanon." *Middle East Report* 162 (January-February 1990) pp. 26-30.

———. "Kamal Jumblatt." In Bernard Reich (Ed.), *Political Leaders of The Contemporary Middle East and North Africa: A Bibliographical Dictionary.* New York: Greenwood Press, 1990, pp. 100-110.

———."Walid Jumblatt." In Bernard Reich (Ed.), *Political Leaders of the Contemporary Middle East and North Africa: A Bibliographical Dictionary.* New York: Greenwood Press, 1990, pp. 115-120.

———. "Political Parties in Underdeveloped Countries: The Case of the Progressive Socialist Party of Lebanon, 1949-1978." Ph.D. diss., George Washington University, 1990.

———. "The Political Economy of Violence: The War-System in Colombia." *Journal of Interamerican Studies and World Affairs* 39, no. 2 (Summer 1997), pp. 37-81.

Rommel, M. Ferdinand. "Ethno-Regionalist Parties in Western Europe: Universe and Electoral Success." Paper presented at the Annual meeting of the American Political Science Association, September 1993.

Rothschild, Joseph. *Ethnopolitics.* New York: Columbia University Press, 1981.

Rudolph, Lloyd, and Susanne Rudolph. *The Modernity of Tradition: Political Development of India.* Chicago: University of Chicago Press, 1967.

Rueschmeyer, Dietrich, Evelyne Stephens, and John Stephens. *Capitalist Development and Democracy.* Chicago: University of Chicago Press, 1992.

Salibi, Kamal. *A House of Many Mansions: The History of Lebanon Revisited.* Berkeley: University of California Press, 1988.

———. *Modern History of Lebanon.* New York: Frederick A. Praeger, 1965.

Sartori, Giovanni. *Party and Party Systems: Framework for Analysis.* vol. 1. Cambridge: Cambridge University Press, 1976.

Scott, Robert. "Parties and Policy-Making." In Joseph LaPalombra and Myron Weiner (Eds.). *Political Parties and Political Development.* Princeton, NJ: Princeton University Press, 1966.

Shanin, Teodor (Ed.). *Peasants and Peasant Societies.* London: Penguin Books, 1984.

Sharabi, Hisham (Ed.). *The Next Arab Decade: Alternative Futures.* Boulder, CO: Westview Press, 1988.

Shemayel, Eve. *Sousiologia al-Nizam al Siyasi al Lubanani* (The Sociology of the Lebanese Political System). n.a: Jameat Grou Noble, n.a.

Skinner, Elliot. "Group Dynamics of Changing Societies: The Problem of Tribal Politics in Africa." In J. Heldi (Ed.). *Essays on the Problem of Tribe.* Seattle: University of Washington Press, 1968.

Sklar, Richard. *Nigerian Political Parties: Power in an Emergent African Nation.* Princeton, NJ: Princeton University Press, 1963.

Smilianskaya, A. M. *Al-Harakat al-Falahiyya Fi Lubnan Fi-Nisf al-Qarn al-Tasei Ashar* (Peasant Movements in Lebanon in the First Half of the Nineteenth Century). Beirut: Dar al-Farabi, 1972.

Suleiman, Michael. "The Lebanese Communist Party." *Middle Eastern Studies* 2 (January 1967), pp. 146-154.

———. *Political Parties in Lebanon: The Challenges of a Fragmented Political Culture.* New York: Cornell University Press, 1967.

Tsebelis, George. *Nested Games: Rational Choice in Comparative Politics.* Berkeley: University of California Press, 1990.

U.K. Public Record Office. 1840. FO 406/8 120631.

U.S. National Archives. SWNCC Country Study on Long-Range Assistance to Lebanon. Document #890 E.00/ 6-848, 1946.

U.S. National Archives. Dispatches U.S. Department of State. Doc. no. 783A.00/2-1952.

Vail, Leroy (Ed.). *The Creation of Tribalism in Southern Africa.* Berkeley: University of California Press, 1989.

Valenzuela, A. *The Breakdown of Democratic Regimes: Chile.* Baltimore: Johns Hopkins University Press, 1987.

Wallerstein, Immanuel. *The Capitalist World-Economy.* London: Cambridge University Press, 1987.

———. *The Modern World System I.* New York: Academic Press, 1974.

———. *The World System III: The Second Era of Great Expansion of the Capitalist World Economy, 1730-1840.* San Diego, CA: Academic Press, 1989.

Waltz, Kenneth. *Theory of International Politics.* Berkeley: University of California Press, 1979.

Wathaek wa Takareer al Sadera an al Moutamar al Watani al Sades lil Hizb al Shioui al Lubnani (Documents and Reports of the Sixth National Conference of the Lebanese Communist Party). Beirut: Lebanese Communist Party, 1992.

Weber, Max. *The Theory of Social and Economic Organization.* London: The Free Press, 1947.

Yamak, Labib Zuwiyya. "Party Politics in the Lebanese Political System." In Leonard Binder (Ed.). *Politics in Lebanon.* New York: John Wiley and Sons, 1966.

Zey, Mary (Ed.). *Decision Making: Alternatives to Rational Choice Models.* Newbury Park, CA: Sage Publications, 1992.

CONSULTED PERIODICALS

Al-Amal, Beirut daily.
Al-Anba, weekly magazine of the Progressive Socialist Party.
Al-Hayyat, London daily.
Al-Nahar, Beirut daily.
Al-Safir, Beirut daily.

INDEX

Akel, Saeed, 72
Albert, Adeeb, 26
Aleily, Abdallah, 36, 38
Arab nationalism, 40-42, 44, 53, 54, 58, 71, 73
  Arab unity, 49
  nationhood, 6
Arislan, 83, 102
Assabiya, 133
al-Assad, Ahmad, 73
Austrian Republic, 7

Baath Party, 16, 71, 74, 86
Baydoun, Rashid, 29
Bechara, el Khouri, 21, 39, 56, 72
Belgium, 7
Berri, Nabih, 102
Birnamej al Islah al-Marjale, 57
Bistani, Fouad, 38
Brown, Roger, 12
Bustani, Emille, 39

Cedar's Quards, 55
Chamoun, Camille, 39-41, 47, 59, 73, 77
Chile, 5, 6
Civil war, 90-92, 125, 126
Colombia, 8, 9
communist, 6, 74, 80, 83, 86, 108-115 (*see also* Lebanese Communist Party)
Communist Work Organization, *see* Organization of Communist Work.
consociationalism, 9, 22, 30, 32, 37, 52, 54, 56, 59, 61, 126, 136-139, 143, 149

democratic breakdown, 2, 45, 46, 56, 57
Dib, Regis, 125, 128
Drucker, Peter, 28

Ecuador, 8
Edde, Boutrus, 39
Edde, Raymond, 59, 97
ethnic conflict, 7-10, 118, 119, 120-122, 141, 144
European Economic Community, 41
European powers, 18

Fadllah, Hussain, 135
Fakhri, Majid, 38

General Confederation of Workers Trade Unions, 149
Germany (Weimar Republic), 7
Gulf War, 136

Hamedeh, Saeed, 38
Hanna, George, 36, 37, 41
Hawi, George, 111, 112
Helf al-Thulathi, 55, 111
Helou, Charles, 50, 57, 78
Horowitz, Donald, 8, 10
Hudson, Michael, 30
Huntington, Samuel, 4
Hussein, Saddam, 11

intrasectarian conflict, 121, 128, 133
Israel, 100, 101
Istfan, Yusuf, 18

Jaber, Shakib, 52
Jubran, Farid, 36, 46, 95
Jumayyel, Amin, 101, 127
Jumayyel, Bashir, 123
Jumayyel, Pierre, 97, 123, 124, 127
Jumblatt, Hikamat, 35
Jumblatt, Kamal, 35, 36, 37, 38, 43, 49, 53, 57, 72, 77, 78, 94, 121
Jumblatt, Nazira, 35
Jumblatt, Walid, 62, 64, 99, 100

Kaimakamieh, 19
Karami, Rashid, 36, 37, 40, 59, 74
Khalaf, Abbas, 36, 46, 52, 95
Khatib, Anwar, 39, 92
Khatib, Zaher, 92

Lebanese Communist Party, 55, 65, 74, 80, 87, 107, 108-115, 136, 138, 139
Lebanese Forces (LF), 100, 101, 121, 128, 129
Lebanese National Movement, 57, 59, 63, 80, 85, 145
Liberation Bloc, 36

Maheiri, Issam, 118
Mainwaring, Scott, 5
Maksoud, Clovis, 41, 52
al-Mithak, 38 (*see also* PSP Modernization Theory)
Moueh, Kareem, 110
Mountain War, 60, 100
Mourabiton Sunni movement, 96
Muhsin, Ibrahim, 110, 113, 125
Mutasarafieh, 19-21

national bloc, 35
National Dialogue Committee, 59, 60, 77
national pact, 21, 23, 33, 38, 136 (*see also* Taif Accord)
Nicaragua, 8
Nigeria, 7, 9

Organization of Communist Work, 57, 63, 83
Ottoman Empire, 20
Oun, Michel, 101, 130-132

Palestine Liberation Organization (PLO), 61, 81, 90, 145
Palestinian resistance, 54, 81
Parkin, Frank, 44
peasant revolts, 17, 18
Perot, Ross, 29
political parties
  Amal Movement, 122, 123
  Kataib Party, 29, 55, 59, 86, 96, 123-129
  Middle East, 3, 4, 10, 11, 12
  National Bloc Party, 59
  National Liberal Party, 59, 60 (*see also* Lebanese Communist Party *and* SSNP)
  Western, 6-8, 27, 28, 29
PSP Modernization Theory, 8

rational choice, 5, 6, 34, 35, 45, 47, 60, 61, 90, 100, 141, 142
Rizk, Fouad, 36, 37, 38

Saad, Maaouf, 80
Saker, Mouris, 41
Salam, Saeb, 40, 59, 73, 78
Salibi, Kamal, 26
Salman, Fouad, 46
Sartori, Giovanni, 144

sectopolitics, 15, 16, 29, 33, 42, 59, 95, 120, 135, 137, 138, 146
sects
  Armenians, 86
  Christian Orthodox, 19, 20, 107, 115
  Druze, 17-21, 24, 63, 102, 103-104
  Maronite, 17-21, 22, 24, 28, 43, 47, 54, 59
  Shiite, 20, 24, 29, 71, 122, 133
  Sunni, 19, 20, 21, 24
Shaheen, Tanious, 18
Shaiban, Shaker, 36, 39
Sheikh al-Akel, 63
Shihab, Bachir, 18
Shihab, Fouad, 49, 51, 76, 78
Six February Revolt, 101
social movements, 148-150
Socialist National Front, 39, 45
Sudan, 10, 11
al-Sulh, Riyadh, 31
Switzerland, 7
Syria, 135, 136, 137
Syrian Social National Party (SSNP), 77, 80, 107, 115-120, 138, 139

Taif Accord, 104, 105, 138, 145, 147
al-Tufaily, Subhi, 134

United States, 7

Valenzuela, Arturo, 56
Venezuela, 5, 7, 150

Waltz, Kenneth, 106, 138
war system, 102
Wasta system, 88-90
Weber, Max, 13, 22, 23, 24
  Weberian, 78